The Cincinnati Zoo
and Botanical Garden

From Past to Present

This book is dedicated to my parents and grandparents. In particular, it is dedicated to my step-grandfather, Perin McDermott. "Mac" told me about his childhood memories of the Cincinnati Zoo at the turn of the century. He especially recalled the Zoo's passenger pigeons and told me that only a few decades earlier, his father had seen passenger pigeons by the millions in southern Ohio. The few passenger pigeons at the Cincinnati Zoo in the early 1900s were the last remaining individuals of this species which was once the most numerous bird on earth. In a larger sense, this book is dedicated to our common human past and to our shared natural heritage.

The publication of
The Cincinnati Zoo and Botanical Garden: From Past to Present
has been made possible through the major support of

Berenfield Containers, Inc.

with additional support from Dr. Emil and Winifred Barrows
and the C. J. Krehbiel Company.

CONTENTS

Foreword

Aside from senior citizen discounts, about the only advantage of growing old is to draw on one's memory of places and events of yesteryear. Thus, I can clearly recall my several visits to the Cincinnati Zoo in the early 1930s.

Surely the Zoo's fortunes were at low ebb at the time. Both the buildings and grounds looked run-down and in need of paint and repair, pruning and fertilizer. Sol Stephan, the grand old man whose name was virtually synonymous with the Zoo, was still presiding over a fine animal collection, but age was sapping his energy and his son, Joseph, was in active charge.

In April, 1992, six decades later, I made my most recent visit, and I was astounded by what I saw. What an extraordinary change, even in the name, which had become the Cincinnati Zoo and Botanical Garden. New or well-kept buildings, innovations in exhibiting livestock, a unique insect house, and the grounds beautifully planted with myriads of spring flowers of many kinds in bloom. The genius, energy, and vivid imagination of Edward J. Maruska, the Zoo's current director, were evident everywhere.

The Cincinnati Zoo, the oldest institution of its kind in America, save for my own "alma mater," has had a long history, many ups and downs, innumerable firsts, and a heritage dating from the many early citizens of German ancestry who, like their compatriots in Europe, had an absorbing interest in nature, the arts, and science. It was inevitable that they should found a zoo in the Queen City of the Ohio River Valley.

David Ehrlinger, the Cincinnati Zoo's outstanding horticulturist, has assembled an exhaustive collection of facts, augmented by a large and truly impressive series of illustrations, chiefly from the zoo archives. With these he has provided us with the most carefully chronicled history I have ever seen about any zoo. I hope you will enjoy reading it as much as I have.

Roger Conant
Director Emeritus,
Philadelphia Zoological Garden, and
Adjunct Professor,
University of New Mexico

Introduction

The Cincinnati Zoo, founded in 1873, stands out among American zoos in its long and rich history. The legacy of the Cincinnati Zoo has been an important one both in the development of American zoos and in the history of the local region. It was the second major zoological garden to be established in America and because of its significant architecture, it is recognized as a National Historic Landmark. Throughout its past the Zoo's architecture and design has been significant. The Zoo's early history was strongly influenced by Cincinnati's German immigrant population and these German influences are unique among American zoos. Furthermore, Sol Stephan, the Superintendent and General Manager from 1886-1937, played a pioneering role in the development of the modern American zoo director.

The Cincinnati Zoo's history is especially difficult to trace because of its long time span, German cultural background, changes in organizational structure, gaps in the archival record, and from the beginning, its complex, multi-dimensional character. This book is the result of several years of interest in zoo history and almost two decades of Cincinnati Zoo employment. My goal has been to produce an interesting, yet meaningful, book, utilizing an extensive selection of photographs and illustrations to amplify the text. Because this is not a comprehensive history, I have had to be especially selective in the contents. At the same time because of space limitations it has been frustrating to have omitted so many of the people, animals, stories, and lore that have been a vital part of the Cincinnati Zoo over the years.

David B. Ehrlinger, Jr.

April 9, 1993

Acknowledgements

I would like to express my appreciation to the many people who have contributed in some way to this book. I have talked to dozens of people about the Cincinnati Zoo in the past few years, all of whom I cannot mention here. I want to especially acknowledge Dr. Judith Spraul-Schmidt, adjunct history faculty member at the University of Cincinnati. Her masters thesis on the Zoo, written in 1977, has been an invaluable resource. She has read several drafts of the book and provided critical comments and encouragement. Walter E. Langsam, architectural historian and teacher at the University of Cincinnati, has provided information and comments based on his extensive local architectural research. He has also graciously edited the text. I would like to thank Dr. Edward Maruska and Dr. Betsy Dresser for reviewing the manuscript and for their comments. Dr. John Clubbe, professor of English at the University of Kentucky and author of *Cincinnati Observed: Architecture and History*, also read the book and gave valuable suggestions and encouragement. I want to express my appreciation to Dr. Roger Conant for his introduction, and also for historical and editorial comments. Elizabeth Kenney provided crucial support throughout the project in both research and editing. Ruth Wilhelmy helped immensely in translating many pages of German text. For their assistance, I am grateful to Brynn Ballou, and Joanna Wright, as well as Steve Feist, who did the studio photography. Ruth Trosset and Nell L. Galloway helped by proofreading and providing other editorial support. I want to thank my wife, Claire, and staff member Debbie Zurieck for their contributions and desktop publishing expertise. In addition, I want to acknowledge the assistance of former staff member Rob Halpern, who is now Curator of Horticulture at the International Wildlife Conservation Park (formerly the New York Zoological Park). John Anderson demonstrated remarkable skill and patience in scanning illustrations as well as providing additional production assistance.

Important sources of information have included Dr. Sol G. Stephan, Tecla B. Stephan, Susan Labry Meyn, and fellow staff members Edward Maruska, Betsy Dresser, Bob Lotshaw, Mike Dulaney, John Arnett, Dave Oehler, Thane Maynard, Tom Penn, Cathryn Hilker, Nora Kelly, and Karen Wachs. Herman Reichenbach, a zoo historian from Hamburg, Germany, has helped me understand several German zoo connections through his correspondence. Other contributions that I would like to acknowledge came from Dr. Harro Strehlow (zoo historian, Berlin, Germany), Marvin Jones (Registrar, the San Diego Zoological Garden), Dr. Cynthia Fields and Heather Ewing (the Office of Architectural History and Historic Preservation, Smithsonian Institution), James Charleton (History Division, National Park Service, U. S. Department of the Interior), Robert D. Powell (Theodore Roosevelt National Park, National Park Service), Steven P. Johnson (Archivist of the International Wildlife Conservation Park), Charlotte Shockley (Archivist of the Cincinnati Opera), Jeanne Segal (Vice-President/Travel, Publications, Volunteer Programs, Philadelphia Zoological Garden), Joyce Shaw and Judy Vismara (Lincoln Park Zoological Garden), David McNeil, Nelson Hoffman, and Fred D. Pfening, III. For other information I also want to thank Carson R. Whiting, Oliver M. Gale, Carl A. Strauss, Hester Stephenson, Henrietta Kueny Price, David Kern, John A. Ruthven, Mary Ellyn Hutton, Charles Parsons, Val Kettering, Mildred Hastings, as well as many others. I would like to acknowledge the assistance of Dr. Don Heinrich Tolzmann (The University of Cincinnati Langsam Library), Ric Hider (the National Zoo), William C. Black (Archivist, The Lloyd Library and Museum), the Field Museum of Natural History library, the library staff of the *Cincinnati Enquirer,* the staff of the Rare Book collection of the Public Library of Cincinnati and Hamilton County, and Linda J. Bailey, Laura L. Chace, Scott Gampher, and other staff of the Cincinnati Historical Society.

Although most photographic materials are from the Cincinnati Zoo archives, a number of photographs and postcards have been used through the generous cooperation of several sister institutions and private individuals. These include: the Cincinnati Art Museum, the *Cincinnati Enquirer*, the Cincinnati Historical Society, the Cincinnati Museum of Natural History, the Cincinnati Opera, the *Cincinnati Post*, the Public Library of Cincinnati and Hamilton County, Hagenbeck's Tierpark, the Lloyd Library and Museum, the Taft Museum, Dr. and Mrs. Sol G. Stephan, Pamela S. Brown, Chuck Bricking, and Paul W. Schuch. Photographic credits are listed on page 134.

The Cincinnati Zoo
and Botanical Garden
From Past to Present

EAGLE CAGE.

RESTAURANT.

ZOOLOGICAL GARDEN.

BEAR PIT.

The Cincinnati Zoological Garden in the late 1880s.

Advertisement.

The Zoo Begins: The 1870s

The origins of the Cincinnati Zoo are connected to the dynamic social, economic, and technological changes that occurred in the middle of the 19th century. Throughout Europe and America. growing urban centers became much more important economically, socially, and culturally. Cincinnati was founded in 1788 along the Ohio River, one of the earliest cities to be established in the Midwest. With its access to steamboat transportation and bolstered by German and Irish immigration, Cincinnati was the fastest growing city in the United States by the middle of the 19th century. After the Civil War it ranked among the nation's leading cities in population, manufacturing, and commerce. Through much of the century the "Queen City of the West" was also the most important cultural center west of the leading eastern cities. Cincinnati, however, was not growing as rapidly as other Midwest cities like Chicago and St. Louis, which caused concern among Cincinnati's civic boosters.

After the Civil War, Cincinnati and other large American cities were being transformed by forces which affected every aspect of urban life. Many of these changes were important in the formation of the modern zoo. Innovation and discovery in science and technology revolutionized life and created popular interest in the sciences, including zoology and botany. Public education became more important. Along with improved education, communication, and commerce there developed a growing interest in foreign peoples, places, and natural history. Improved urban transportation, including cable cars, inclines, and electric trolleys, allowed cities to grow larger and radically changed the locations and relationships of urban institutions, residences, and workplaces. For most Americans the standard of living had greatly improved by the late 1800s.

During this period urban society was changing. Recreation became more important for all classes of people as the work week gradually shortened. The middle and upper classes expanded in size and influence. Leading citizens promoted education, culture, and the arts as a means of uplifting urban life. Across America they organized cultural and educational institutions, expositions, and festivals in leading cities. In Cincinnati a number of institutions were founded, both as a consequence of the city's cultural development and to boost its declining urban status. Cincinnati was fortunate in having a number of public-minded benefactors who founded such cultural institutions as Music Hall, the May Festival, the College of Music, the Cincinnati Art Museum and Academy, and the University of Cincinnati, in addition to the Cincinnati Zoological Garden. Other educational and scientific institutions like the Public Library, the Society of Natural History (today's Cincinnati Museum of Natural History), and the Historical and Philosophical Society of Ohio (today's Cincinnati Historical Society) also developed in this energetic and inspired era.

By the mid-1800s American cities began to provide new municipal services and expand traditional ones. Education, public health, water and sewer systems, as well as police and fire protection, developed as governmental services. Scenic public parks, created by skilled landscape designers, became another new municipal service for urban populations living in crowded, polluted cities. In Cincinnati spacious new parks were created by the noted German-born landscape designer, Adolph Strauch, who was the superintendent of Cincinnati's Spring Grove Cemetery and the city's parks.

The Entrance to the Cincinnati Zoological Garden.

The Zoo's Origins

After 1830 the population of Cincinnati grew rapidly through German immigration. These new citizens became an important part of the city's economic, social, and cultural life. They created a rich and picturesque urban culture which gave Cincinnati a special character and vitality and catalyzed the city's cultural development. Most of the Germans lived in the Over-the-Rhine district, a community north of downtown, filled with Germanic culture and vitality.

A burst of scientific and cultural activities arose in the mid-1800s throughout German-speaking Europe. Among these were the earliest German zoological gardens. Beginning with the Berlin Zoological Garden in 1844, a number of larger German cities established zoological gardens, as did other major European cities. Prominent figures involved in the new German zoos included explorer-naturalist Alexander von Humboldt, philosopher Arthur Schopenhauer, landscape designer Peter Lenné, and members of the aristocracy. These zoological gardens followed the earliest public European zoos of the era: Vienna's Tierpark Schoenbrunn (opened to the public in 1765), the Ménagerie du Jardin des Plantes in Paris (opened in 1793), and the London Zoological Garden (opened in 1828). The new zoological gardens were different from the earlier animal menageries with their small cages. Animals were displayed in larger public garden settings. Exhibits were aesthetically placed in landscaped parks among planted trees and shrubs, existing woodlands, ponds, and streams. The significance of this park or garden setting is reflected in the term "zoological garden." Zoological gardens contained much larger collections of animals, representing the range of the animal kingdom. They were displayed in larger, more spacious exhibits, organized according to zoological taxonomy, and labeled for educational benefit and study. Animals were given as much space as possible and the exhibits were intended to be naturalistic in design. As products of 19th-century concepts of science and beauty, these early zoological gardens recreated a tamed, controlled Garden of Eden in which many species of animals and plants were carefully maintained for the educational, scientific, and cultural benefit of human society.

Members of Cincinnati's German community had visited the new zoological gardens of Europe and wanted to establish a similar facility locally. They admired the scientific, educational, aesthetic, and recreational values of these new public institutions. In 1873 a local newspaper stated, "... the importance of such institutions for science and general cultivation has long been recognized...." The article went on to point out that regarding children, "For general instruction there can hardly be a better school than a zoological garden...."

Cincinnati's scientific community looked forward to the new zoological garden. The *Cincinnati Quarterly Journal of Science* applauded the zoological garden as a "medium to advance the knowledge of natural science, and to give to the great masses a place for genial amusement combined with elevating observation of the animal and vegetable kingdoms." A number of the city's native-born community leaders were also supporters of the new zoological garden. Many were involved in the city's other cultural institutions and activities. They included such prominent local figures as art patron Joseph Longworth, his son-in-law George Ward Nichols, department store owner John Shillito, businessman Charles Phelps Taft, steel magnate George K. Shoenberger, businessman John Simpkinson, businessman Julius Dexter, and circus owner John Robinson. Robinson, who owned the Robinson Circus, had advocated for some time establishing a "grand" zoological garden in Cincinnati that would promote the city and attract visitors.

Souvenir album illustration (1880s).

The Founding of the Zoo

In the early 1870s there were no major European-style zoological gardens in the United States, although New York's small Central Park Zoo, which opened by 1864, and Chicago's Lincoln Park Zoological Garden, which opened in 1868, displayed small collections of animals. On July 1, 1874 the Philadelphia Zoological Garden opened. It was the first major zoological garden in the U.S.A. with a zoological society that had been earlier chartered in 1859. It was 33 acres with a comprehensive design that was largely patterned after the London Zoological Garden. In the early 1870s in Cincinnati a wealthy German immigrant and a life-long animal lover, Andrew (Andreas) Erkenbrecher, was discussing with his business associates founding a major zoological garden. Compared to the Philadelphia Zoological Garden, Cincinnati's zoo would have a stronger Germanic influence in its origin, design, operations, and collections.

In 1872 Cincinnati experienced a widespread outbreak of caterpillars which defoliated the city's trees. In response Andrew Erkenbrecher, who owned one of the nation's largest starch manufacturing companies, organized a group of leading citizens to form the Society for the Acclimatization of Birds. In order to control insects, the Society imported hundreds of insect-eating European species, including starlings and English sparrows. Similar introductions were, unfortunately, made by other well-meaning acclimatization groups in eastern cities, so that starlings and English sparrows soon became established in North America.

In 1873 Andrew Erkenbrecher directed the secretary of the Acclimatization Society to write to the renowned German zoologist and zoo director, Dr. Alfred Brehm, for information on establishing a zoological garden. Erkenbrecher read Brehm's encouraging response at an Acclimatization Society meeting in June and proposed that a zoological society be formed to establish a large zoological garden in Cincinnati. There was enthusiastic response and on July 11, 1873, the Zoological Society of Cincinnati was incorporated as a joint stock company for profit, patterned after similar European institutions. Its purpose was "... the study and dissemination of a knowledge of the nature and habits of the creatures of the animal kingdom." According to the first Annual Report, " the object of the Society is to establish a garden which will be a profit to the stockholders, a credit to the city, and a continual source of improvement to its visitors." The nine members of the Society's Board of Directors were prominent citizens, both native-born and German immigrants. Many of them served on the boards of the city's other cultural institutions. The Board's first officers

Andrew Erkenbrecher was the founder of the Cincinnati Zoo. A German immigrant, he was known for his personal warmth, enthusiasm, vision, and determination. (From the Collection of the Public Library of Cincinnati and Hamilton County)

were: Joseph Longworth, President; John Simpkinson, Vice-President; Clemens Oskamp, Treasurer; Charles Phelps Taft, Recording Secretary; and Armin Tenner, Corresponding Secretary. A capitalization of $300,000, consisting of 6,000 shares of $50 each, was authorized. Later Armin Tenner was sent to Germany to try to hire Dr. Alfred Brehm to direct Cincinnati's zoo. Although an offer was apparently made to Brehm, later in September an international business panic or crash struck. Because of this and a recession that followed, the proposed $300,000 of capitalization was scaled back due to a lack of investors. Negotiations with Brehm also evidently ended and no further progress was made on the Zoo for six months.

Andrew Erkenbrecher (1821-1885) was the founder of the Cincinnnati Zoo. He was remembered long after for his personal warmth, self-effacing nature, vision, determination, and enthusiastic support for the Zoo. According to an early Board officer, the origin of the Zoo was "chiefly due to the extraordinary labor" of Erkenbrecher. His remarkable efforts and character were undoubtedly instrumental in the establishment of a major zoological garden in Cincinnati, earlier than other comparable American cities with large German populations.

Site Selection and Design

The Cincinnati Zoological Garden was ambitiously conceived by its founders on a comprehensive scale, carefully integrating inspired architecture and landscape design with a large animal collection. It was planned on a larger scale than the 33 acres of Philadelphia's zoo. It would be located on an attractive hilly, wooded setting and be comparable in size with the largest European zoological gardens. A scenic site with varied topography would be selected and would include ponds, streams, and level pastures for animal exhibits. One of the Zoo's founders, Armin Tenner, who had toured European zoos, reported in 1873 that "the cage system began to be abolished and the animals were housed in as natural a manner as possible..." with "... the largest possible liberty...." While the design of exhibits in the leading zoos of the times attempted to be naturalistic both aesthetically and philosophically, by today's standards the early caging and fencing technology greatly limited naturalism.

Cincinnati's two major parks were considered as sites because of their scenic beauty. The newly opened Eden Park was dismissed, however, because of its lack of large trees. Earlier, its

Deer Park. Spacious areas for deer, called deer parks, were common in Europe in both zoos and large private estates. This lithograph from an 1878 souvenir album shows the rolling terrain that was an important part in the site selection of the Zoo.

slopes had been covered by Nicholas Longworth's extensive vineyards. The unfinished southern section of the new Burnet Woods park seemed a better choice because of its existing woodlands. Cincinnati Park Superintendent Adolph Strauch approved of the choice. Strauch had designed many of the estate landscapes in the fashionable, neighboring suburb of Clifton and was internationally renowned as a landscape designer. For the new zoological garden Strauch recommended that a landscape designer be hired, that the woodlands be preserved, and that an experimental garden be added as well. Although the City Council also approved leasing the Burnet Woods site, the Mayor vetoed the proposal because of reservations about turning over such a valuable tract of land to a private enterprise without more city control. This section of Burnet Woods later became part of the campus of the University of Cincinnati.

Eagle and Owl Pavilion and the Squirrel House. This lithograph shows the Zoo's first bird of prey exhibits and a smaller "Squirrel House" on the left.

After a careful search, a nearby site called Blakely Woods, located in the suburb of Avondale, was selected. Then used as a dairy cow pasture, the site's partially wooded 66 acres consisted of the appropriate scenic features: rolling hills, ravines, streams, and small ponds. The property, which was three miles from downtown, was leased on September 24, 1874, for 99 years with an option to buy. Rent was $5,000 a year for the first five years, $6,000 for the next five, and $7,500 a year thereafter.

In the fall of 1874 Theodor Findeisen, a landscape gardener-engineer, was hired to situate buildings, exhibits, walkways, and plantings. Findeisen had had experience in similar work in Europe. His design of the Zoological Garden harmoniously used the natural features of the site, creating a pastoral landscape with a succession of picturesque focal points and visual experiences, including ravines, streams, tree groves, vistas, animal exhibits, and architecture. Extensive grading and other enhancements of the site were accomplished to create " a delightful park, where hill and vale, grassy lawn, and blue lakelet, flashing cascade, and rustic bridge will alternate in attracting the eye, forming vistas of varied beauty...." (The *Cincinnati Quarterly Journal of Science*, Jan. 1875). At the center of the Zoo was a pond, which was enlargened by an earth dam and extensive excavation. Findeisen's work was considered "a masterpiece of modern landscape gardening" by experts of the day. Findeisen's pathway design was similar to the curvilinear layouts of zoological gardens in Frankfurt, Berlin, and Hamburg. This circulation route consisted of a circular-shaped roadway around the perimeter of the grounds that was wide enough for the carriages of wealthy patrons, along with an interconnecting network of narrow footpaths. Much of Findeisen's original design is preserved in the layout of today's Zoo. In contrast, however, many of Findeisen's recommendations regarding building and exhibit placement were rejected. At the end of 1874 Findeisen was dismissed by the Board for unknown reasons and construction came to a halt during the winter.

Rustic bridge and walkways in the late 1870s. The visitor soon discovers "... pretty vistas arising from this skillful plan of the original designer...." Supplement to the Scientific American, *June 3, 1919. (Courtesy of The Cincinnati Historical Society)*

Curt Terne from Savannah, Georgia, was hired as a temporary Superintendent in the fall of 1874. After working for three months with Theodor Findeisen on the Zoo's layout and early construction, Terne was dismissed. The Society then sent its German-born agent, Armin Tenner, to Europe to hire a permanent superintendent and to study leading European zoological gardens. The recently completed Frankfurt Zoo was admired as a model for further design of Cincinnati's zoological garden, even though the Cincinnati Zoo was twice as large and had a hillier, more attractive site. Dr. H. Dorner, the Scientific-Secretary of the Hamburg Zoological Garden, was selected as the Zoo's first permanent Superintendent. He started on April 24, 1875, at a salary of $3,000 a year plus house rent. The Cincinnati Zoo followed the German practice of hiring a professional director or superintendent who possessed a scientific doctorate degree. The Cincinnati Zoo's Superintendent generally directed operations, although decisions about policy, purchases, and contracts had to be approved by the Board of Directors. Superintendent Dorner was responsible for acquiring a comprehensive animal collection and played an important role in the location and construction of the animal exhibits and buildings. Most of the decisions concerning layout and construction, however, were placed in the hands of a Board committee, composed of Andrew Erkenbrecher, Julius Dexter, and John Simpkinson.

Hoofed animal displays were generally large in size. Some were located on level plateaus that suggested the plains and savannah habitats of many exhibited animals. In the foreground of this lithograph is the Deer House with the Ostrich House in the background.

Enhancing Nature

The full range of the property's varied topography was used in locating the Zoo's exhibits and buildings. According to the *Cincinnati Commercial* "all avenues, roads, and walks were laid out with regard to the natural disposition of the land." The pond was enlarged in the fall of 1874 to exhibit more waterfowl and islands were added to enhance breeding. Existing streams and ravines were utilized for the display of otters, beaver, waterfowl, and for a goldfish pool. Streams and ravines were picturesquely landscaped with naturalistic additions of limestone slabs and other rocks. The most dramatic of these was a large ravine with a fifty-foot cascade. Throughout the Zoo scenic vistas were carefully created and preserved. Existing groves of trees and wooded areas were blended with lawns and undulating hills to create a gentle, pastoral park landscape. The lawns were created from the property's earlier pasturelands. Animal exhibits were made as large as possible, considering the limitations of 19th century technology. Level meadows were often selected for hoofed animal exhibits because they suggested the animals' native plains and savannahs. The steep slope of a hillside was apparently chosen for the bears to evoke the wild mountainous haunts of the animals. Other exhibits were located at periodic intervals throughout the grounds, presumably to maintain the public's interest during the visit and to enhance visual appearances. A spring by the Zoo's entrance was utilized to refresh visitors. There a spring house was built and a stone slab was placed, inscribed with a poem in German. The romantic-style poem, which lauded the merits of water and wine, had been used similarly at the Frankfurt Zoological Garden.

Ravine and cascade. This picturesque feature was enhanced by adding limestone rock walls and ledges to an existing fifty-foot ravine. Within three years it was used as an exhibit for aoudad or Barbary sheep. This large-scale man-made rock feature predated the concrete artificial rockwork exhibits of 20th-century zoos. (Courtesy of The Cincinnati Historical Society)

Eagle and Owl Pavilion. Animal exhibits were picturesque focal points in an informal landscape of existing trees and undulating hilly lawns. (Compare this photograph with the lithograph on page 6.) (Courtesy of The Cincinnati Historical Society)

Beaver Pond (stereograph photograph from the late 1870s). The early Zoo used existing streams and ponds to create naturalistic exhibits for aquatic animals. (Courtesy of The Cincinnati Historical Society)

Zoo Architecture

The Zoo hired Cincinnati architect James W. McLaughlin to design and supervise the construction of all of the Zoo's buildings, except for the already completed Buffalo House. McLaughlin was then one of the area's leading architects and is still considered one of Cincinnati's most outstanding. He designed the Cincinnati Art Museum and Art Academy, a number of major downtown buildings, as well as projects for Zoo founder Andrew Erkenbrecher and other Zoo Board members. McLaughlin demonstrated a range of architectural styles at the Zoo, creating a wide variety of structures from the massive Carnivora House and Restaurant down to small exhibit buildings, a bandstand, and restrooms. In these designs detailed drawings and plans of many European zoo buildings were utilized. McLaughlin worked closely with Superintendent Dorner regarding siting, construction, and the interior design of buildings for the needs of animals.

Construction of the Zoo's major buildings began in May, 1875. The estimated cost of the Zoo's original buildings was $80,000, while pathways and extensive grading was another $40,000. The Zoo's founder, Andrew Erkenbrecher, followed the work closely, visiting the site almost every day. In addition to the skilled tradesmen involved in construction, hundreds of laborers worked for months at $1.50 a day, grading and excavating for paths, buildings, and exhibits.

The Bear Pits were designed according to European models and located on the north slope of a steep hill that suggested the bears' mountainous habitats. The Zoo's informal landscape utilized existing trees, ponds, and the hilly terrain. These lithographs in an 1878 souvenir album depict many of the Zoo's visitors as well-to-do, refined members of society.

Aviaries. This lithograph from an early souvenir album shows these Japanese-style buildings and their large outdoor cages, which housed much of the Zoo's large bird collection. The aviaries were similar to the Indian-style aviaries of the Berlin Zoological Garden. One of Cincinnati's aviaries has been preserved as today's Passenger Pigeon Memorial.

The Cincinnati Zoological Garden's public and exhibit buildings were designed as picturesque focal points in the landscape. The Zoo followed the practice of European zoos and used an eclectic assortment of architectural styles including Gothic, Japanese, Middle Eastern, Teutonic, and rustic. The exotic architecture represented the indigenous buildings of the regions from which exhibited animals originated. It was thought at the time that architectural beauty was enhanced by symbolical allusions that were decoratively incorporated into the structures of the buildings. According to a newspaper, the buildings "... will be in appearance suggestive of the representative countries from which the animals inhabiting them come. For instance, the camel house will be in the shape of a tent, the buffalo house will be built of logs, and so on. They will be arranged to meet the best and most natural comfort of the animals in them." The Japanese style of the seven Aviary buildings was similar to Indian-style aviaries at the Berlin Zoological Garden. One of Cincinnati's original pagoda-style structures has been preserved as today's Passenger Pigeon Memorial building. The Monkey House (today's Reptile House)

Ostrich House. This building sheltered several species of plant-eating animals, including llamas. The design with its "gingerbread" roof trim was similar to German zoo architecture of the time.

Buffalo House. This rustic-style wooden structure used tree branches and bark attached to the walls to evoke the wild origins of animals. It was the Zoo's first building and the only major building not designed by James McLaughlin. Within twenty years it burned down. (Courtesy of The Cincinnati Historical Society)

was described as being of "Turkish" style, while the airy interior was encircled by elegant Corinthian columns. The Reptile House is today the oldest existing zoo building in America. It and the Passenger Pigeon Memorial building as well as the later Elephant House are listed on the National Register of Historic Places and were important in the Cincinnati Zoo's designation in 1987 as a National Historic Landmark.

The architecture was intended to express nature, using organic forms in its structural features. Natural materials were featured to portray the essential character of the zoological garden as a place and as an institution. Massive limestone block walls were used to suggest geological landforms. Large boulders in the bear exhibits dramatically evoked the animals' wild mountainous origins. Rustic log and rock bridges were built throughout the Zoo. Log construction and thatched reed roofs were used at the Deer House. Branches and bark covered the walls of the Buffalo House and represented the native haunts of animals exhibited there. Unfortunately, one of the first residents of the building, "Conqueror," a bull African elephant, did not appreciate the architectural symbolism of his quarters. A few weeks after the Zoo opened, Conqueror began tearing the building down, "...waving the walls and doors around with his trunk...."

In its comprehensive design the Cincinnati Zoological Garden displayed the art and craft of the late 19th century. The latest in scientific and industrial technology was utilized, including elaborate iron and steel caging structures. Large wire-mesh cages allowed many birds room to fly. The outdoor monkey cage, attached to the Monkey House, was almost thirty feet tall, remarkably spacious for zoo exhibits of the time.

The largest of the Zoo's public buildings were constructed of grey limestone and given prominent locations within the grounds. The Monkey House (today's Reptile House) and the Carnivora House were located on scenic vantage points with vistas of the surrounding countryside. The Zoo's largest building, the Restaurant or "Clubhouse," was placed at the center of the Zoo, next to the small lake. The Clubhouse was a monumental three-story Italianate structure with verandas and a grand staircase. From the spacious verandas patrons and visitors could leisurely view much of the Zoo grounds, surveying a selection of both the world's animal life and its vernacular architecture. Like comparable facilities at major German zoos, the Clubhouse served as an important civic center for many

THE RESTAURANT, ZOOLOGICAL GARDENS.

The Restaurant or "Clubhouse" was designed by James McLaughlin and completed in 1876. Patterned after similar facilities at German zoos, this monumental building served as an important civic center for many decades.

years with fine dining, meeting, and entertainment accommodations for up to fifteen hundred people. It stood where the southern part of the Children's Zoo is located today. Built at a cost of $28,000, the Clubhouse was so expensive that it was not finished until September 1876, a year after the Zoo opened. With the opening of the Clubhouse the original plan of the Cincinnati Zoological Garden was completed at a final cost of over $260,000.

Deer House. This shelter house represented the forest habitats of the animals with its log construction and thatched roof and displayed Teutonic architectural styles common in German zoos. (From the Collection of The Public Library of Cincinnati & Hamilton County)

ELEVATION

Aviary Building. Architect James McLaughlin later revised this exotic design and the
Aviary Building instead became the Monkey House, which opened in 1875. Then, as now,
alterations in zoo design were made according to changes in taste, function, and finances.

The Monkey House, now the Reptile House, is the oldest existing zoo building in America and is listed on the National Register of Historic Places.

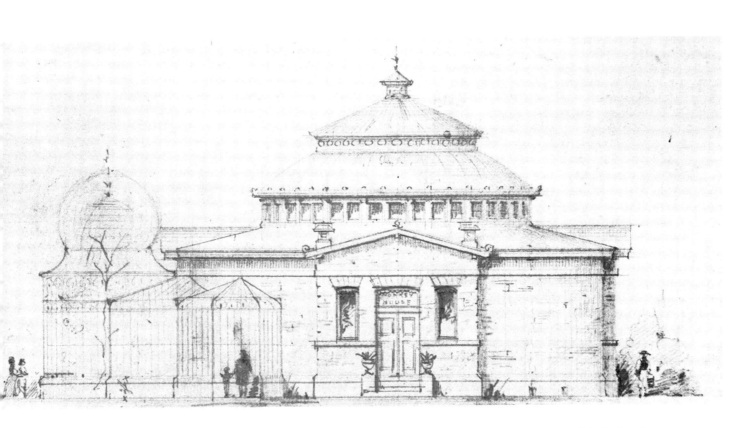

The Monkey House was built in 1875 with a design by James McLaughlin that was described as being of Turkish style. A spacious, thirty-foot-tall monkey cage was attached to the building. Its bulbous shape was similar to the design of the dome of the proposed Aviary building (see the sketch on the facing page).

The Animals and Opening Day

From the start the Zoo's founders attempted to display a comprehensive collection of animals. Although $50,000 was initially allocated for animal purchases, the Zoo later reduced the amount to $20,000. This was apparently due to a lack of funding and also to a new 20% duty that had been levied on imported animals. Zoo Superintendent Dorner spent most of the funds purchasing animals from Carl Hagenbeck, a young animal dealer who was also from Hamburg, Germany. Hagenbeck later became the leading dealer in the world. He and his sons established a close relationship with the Cincinnati Zoo that continued for more than 75 years.

Other purchases included a variety of relatively inexpensive western native animals as well as a bull African elephant, and some animals from a small bankrupt circus. The spirited elephant was delivered by a young man whose handling skills were so valuable that Zoo President Julius Dexter offered him a job. The young man, Salvator "Sol" Stephan, stayed sixty-two years and directed the Zoo's operations from 1886 to 1937.

Many citizens donated a wide array of animals. Andrew Erkenbrecher contributed much of his extensive bird and purebred dog collection. New York's Central Park Menagerie donated a bald eagle. Carl Hagenbeck donated a pair of young olive baboons. The Cincinnati Park Board donated a golden eagle and five white-tailed deer. Adolph Strauch continued his support, contributing pairs of owls, mute swans, and Canada geese. Strauch was a noted bird breeder and the first to breed the once endangered trumpeter swans of North America, the largest species of swan. He raised over fifty birds and exchanged them throughout this country and Europe, including the London Zoological Garden.

Several months before the Zoo opened, a lioness escaped from her cage and attacked a donkey. The donkey valiantly fought back and after a furious battle the lioness retreated. A couple of laborers attempted to corner the lioness but were bitten and clawed, though not seriously. The lioness was then shot by another worker. The story made international news and the donkey was given hero's honors. The donkey, however, died several months later of its wounds. Both the lioness and the donkey were mounted and exhibited in the Carnivora House for a number of years. Many versions of the story were told around Cincinnati for years. A few days after the Zoo opened a leopard also escaped and was later shot.

The Cincinnati Zoological Garden opened on September 18, 1875, fourteen months after the Philadelphia Zoo. The *Cincinnati Commercial* announced, "Today the Cincinnati Zoological Garden will at last be thrown open to the public and the day will mark yet another epoch in our city's development." Another newspaper described the Zoo as "a thing of big proportions, of splendid landscape work, of splendid buildings, numerous lakes, noble trees, graceful slopes, and splendid specimens of the animal kingdom."

On the Zoo's opening day only a few of the buildings and exhibits were completed because of construction delays due to an unusually rainy summer. Eager stockholders were impatient, however, and wanted to see the Zoo open before another year passed. According to the *Cincinnati Commercial,* "The air was raw and chilling and the people who had the good judgment to wear their shawls and overcoats were by far the happiest and most comfortable on the grounds." The *Cincinnati Enquirer* reported that "such a rare collection of animals is not to be found anywhere else on this continent." Because several of the buildings were not finished, many animals were still in crates and small cages. The highlights of opening day were the monkeys, birds, and a large number of tame deer of various species. On the other hand, the *Cincinnati Commercial* described the yaks as "...pleasant, cow-like personages, that seemed too highly honored by the attention and space bestowed upon them." The article continued "The lions, tigers, and other heavy biters are still in their cages and don't like it a bit." Ducks, geese, and swans could not be released to the Zoo's lake because it was occupied by a six-foot alligator which had escaped from its exhibit. After several days, keeper Sol Stephan finally succeeded in capturing the 'gator. Many animals had not yet been delivered and for several weeks animal shipments kept arriving. Fortunately, all of the exhibit buildings were completed in the next few months.

Later in December the Zoo purchased more animals from the auction of P.T. Barnum's Hippodrome in Connecticut. By the end of

Carnivora House. Many of the Zoo's carnivorous mammals were displayed in this large building. Significant animals that died were also mounted and exhibited here.

1875 the Zoo's animal collection was a respectable one for that time. It included four bear species, thirteen species of monkeys, five deer species, three species of kangaroos, six lions, two tigers, a leopard, a caracal, a cougar, three spotted hyenas, a wombat, a tapir, three bison, 58 prairie dogs, two alligators, ten breeds of pedigreed dogs, an African elephant, and 84 species of birds. There was a total of 769 animals, comprising 259 mammals, 494 birds (including 200 pigeons), and 16 reptiles.

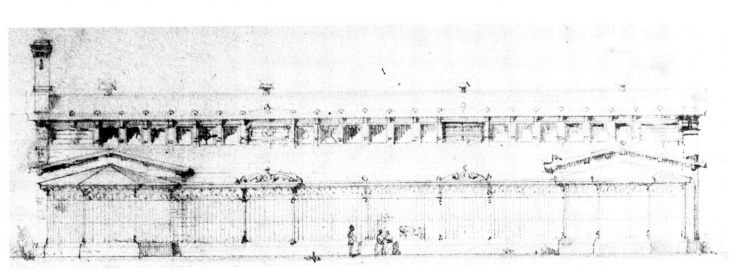

Carnivora House. This was the largest of the Zoo's original exhibit buildings. It was 125 feet long, 60 feet wide, and cost over $19,000. Its design by James McLaughlin was similar to the carnivora buildings of European zoos.

Bird Cage. *The Zoo's founder, Andrew Erkenbrecher, donated this cage to the Zoo along with a large collection of birds and purebred dogs. The cage, originally built in 1868, was used at the Zoo for many years to commemorate Erkenbrecher.*

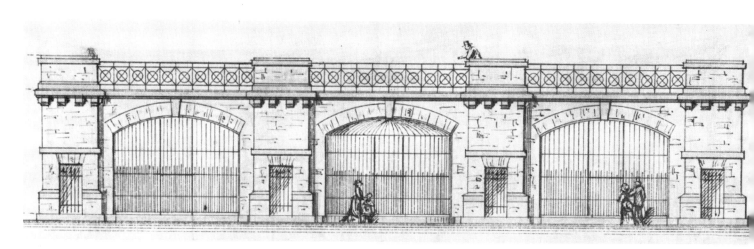

Bear Pits. *This design by James McLaughlin was based on similar exhibits in European zoos. (From the Collection of the Public Library of Cincinnati and Hamilton County)*

Squirrel House. This sketch shows one of several small exhibits that were constructed for small-sized animals. Noted architect James McLaughlin designed a range of animal exhibit buildings.

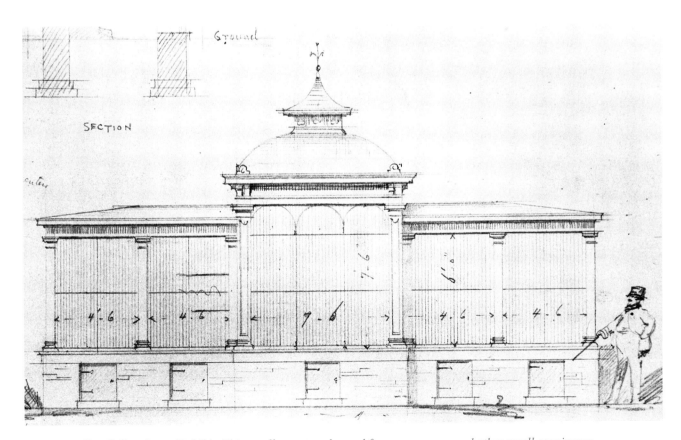

Small Carnivora Exhibit. This small structure housed foxes, raccoons, and other small carnivores.

Ticket Office. Architect James McLaughlin designed a wide range of zoo buildings. His architectural sketches often included people and animals.

Zoo Operations

The Cincinnati Zoological Garden opened with an admission charge of 25 cents for adults and 15 cents for children, while an individual season pass cost six dollars. The child's rate was later reduced to 10 cents. Today these amounts sound inexpensive, but in 1875 a worker made less than $50 a month, working a 55-hour week. These admission rates remained the same for many decades. In order to reduce mounting debts the Zoo stockholders in 1876 voted to assess themselves 50% on their stock. Attendance that year was 102,000. The weather during that first full year of operations was unusually hot, keeping many people away. In 1877 attendance rose to 137,000. In following years Zoo attendance rose when the city hosted large-scale expositions, conventions, and festivals. In 1877, flower beds were added throughout the grounds, and 2,500 trees and

shrubs were planted. Spring Grove Cemetery donated many of the trees, while its famed Superintendent, Adolph Strauch, provided advice. The following year Strauch continued the task of designing and directing the landscaping of the Zoo grounds.

The word "zoo" was first used in a popular British music hall song in 1877 called "Walking in the Zoo is the OK Thing to Do" and referred to the London Zoological Garden. The term "zoo" soon came to be a popular nickname for zoological gardens throughout Europe and North America. In Cincinnati the first guidebook was called "Zoo-Zoo." It was published in 1876 and written by Armin Tenner, the Zoological Garden's former agent and an early interim superintendent.

Outdoor bird exhibit (with the Aviaries and Carnivora House in the background). In 1877 noted landscape designer Adolph Strauch, Superintendent of Spring Grove Cemetery, directed the planting of thousands of trees and shrubs throughout the grounds, including the animal exhibits.

Sea Lion Pool. In 1878 a baby California sea lion was born, evidently the first to be conceived and born in captivity. The exhibit was built in 1877 and has been rebuilt several times over the years. Today the Walrus Exhibit is located on this site.

In 1877 John Robinson, owner of the Robinson Circus of nearby Terrace Park, lent the Zoo a very rare Indian rhinoceros for a year because it proved to be too heavy to transport by wagon on the rickety bridges and muddy roads of the time. The following year the circus decided to travel by train and so the Zoo lost the female rhino. A pony track was added in 1877 and remained a popular feature with children for many years. In 1878 a pair of giraffes was purchased. The female was called "Daisy" and the male was named "Abe," after Abraham Lincoln. In 19th century zoos both giraffes and rhinos were exceedingly rare. A sea lion pool, sixty feet in diameter, was built near the Clubhouse in 1877. The 1877 Annual Report boasted, "Although they [sea lions] cost nearly a thousand dollars, and the pool as much more, the Society has the satisfaction of knowing that they possess the largest Sea Lion tank and the finest specimens on exhibition in the world." The following year a baby California sea lion was born, evidently the first to be conceived and born in captivity. It lived only three or four months, however. Several different sea lion exhibits have been built and rebuilt on this site over the years. Today it is the location of the walrus exhibit. Several of the Zoo's exhibits have had a similar history of construction, demolition, and reconstruction, while retaining the exhibit's basic identity over time.

Since its beginning, transportation issues have always been important to the Zoo. The Zoo's 1874 Annual Report stated, "The grounds are more remote from the City than could have been wished, but they are not too far from it." Progress was made when the Mt. Auburn Street Railway lines were extended to within a half mile of the Zoo entrance. According to a local newspaper, in addition to private carriages, "hired rigs, from the most elaborate carriages down to the humble covered express wagons" brought people to the Zoo.

Nineteenth-century German zoological gardens had a tradition of featuring musical concerts. The young Cincinnati Zoo followed this Old World custom of blending art and nature. As at major German zoos, the Cincinnati Zoo's bandstand was located by the Restaurant. Cincinnati was then one of the musical centers of the nation and its German population was especially known for its love of music. In the summer, families came to the Zoo, enjoyed a meal, and listened to evening or Sunday afternoon musical performances. One of the first concert bands at the Zoo was the German Kaiser's band, which visited soon after the opening, "brilliantly uniformed in immaculate white." The Zoo's early music was directed toward both the cultivated tastes of the upper classes and the popular favorites of the working classes. In the fall of 1875 Sunday concerts featured either grand concerts by the Cincinnati Orchestra's Reed Band for the sophisticated or on alternate weekends popular music for the masses, performed by German bands. Later another favorite band was the Currier military band, composed of Civil War regimental band members. Thousands flocked to the Zoo to hear the band's many concerts of patriotic music.

The Restaurant and lake were focal points at the center of the Zoo. Strollers could promenade around the lake or pause to enjoy the vistas.

The Buffalo House with the Zoo Entrance in the background is depicted in this lithograph from an 1878 souvenir album.

CARNIVORA . AVIARIES .
DOG KENNEL .
BIRDS-EYE VIEW OF CINCINNATI ZOOLOGICAL GARDEN .
MONKEY HOUSE . RESTAURANT . LAKE . ELEPHANT & BUFFALO
DEER PARK . HOUSE .
ENTRANCE . CARRIAGE STANDS .

The Zoo in 1878, a bird's-eye view or panoramic map.

A Unique Legacy

The Cincinnati Zoological Garden was unique among American zoos that were founded in the 19th century. Because of its strong German influences it developed a special character in its original design, collections, and operations that continued for many years. In 1875 German immigrant and physician Dr. Adolph Zipperlen wrote an article describing the Cincinnati Zoological Garden in the prestigious German zoo journal, *Der Zoologische Garten*. He reported, "Although Americans are participating, it is mainly a German project, supported and pushed along by them, and they can be proud to have founded the first zoological garden in the 'West.' Its natural beauty and scenery is outstanding and the layout and the solid buildings are admired by everyone." Zipperlen continued to correspond with the German journal on behalf of the Cincinnati Zoological Garden for over twenty-five years. He later became a Board member, occasionally gave medical advice regarding the Zoo's animals, and wrote a number of German-language articles about the Zoo and its animals. He advocated that animal exhibits be as naturalistic as possible and promoted an active animal breeding program. Zipperlen also urged that the local schools, as in Germany, use the Zoo as an important educational resource. Throughout its early decades the Cincinnati Zoological Garden was an important link for American zoos with the older zoos of Germany and Europe.

The founding of the Cincinnati Zoological Garden was a reflection of the Western world's late 19th-century understanding and vision of the natural world and its human connections. The design of the Zoo integrated aesthetics and science, blending an outstanding animal collection with sophisticated architectural and landscape design. For almost twenty-five years the Cincinnati Zoological Garden and the Philadelphia Zoological Garden remained the largest, most comprehensive, and most costly North American zoos until the New York Zoological Park later opened in 1899.

CARNIVORA.

LAKE.   RESTAURANT.

Zoo scenes in a souvenir album from the late 1880s.

Early Years: The 1880s

In 1885 the Cincinnati Zoo's founder, Andrew Erkenbrecher, died at the age of 63. Called "the Father of the Zoo," his vision, determination, and enthusiasm had brought the Zoological Garden into being. A major problem for the early Zoo was the rapid turnover of Superintendents. There were four Superintendents and four temporary or interim Superintendents in the Zoo's first twelve years. Dr. H. Dorner of Hamburg, Germany, who opened the Zoo in 1875, was discharged after one year for reasons now unknown. Armin Tenner, the Zoo's General Agent, who had hired Dorner, replaced him as interim Superintendent but resigned after a few weeks. H. P. Ingalls served less than a year before ill health forced him to resign. Sea lion expert Frank J. Thompson took over as interim Superintendent. He was later named Superintendent and Secretary, serving seven years before resigning in 1885. The Zoo's Head Gardener, William Bebb, served as an interim Superintendent until the following year when the head keeper, Sol Stephan, was appointed Superintendent. During this tumultuous period the Zoo abandoned the European practice of hiring a zoo director with a scientific doctorate degree, a pattern it had originally followed. Sol Stephan, who was then 37 years old, made up for the previous lack of continuity, directing the Zoo's operations until his retirement in 1937 at the age of 88.

Sol (Salvator) A. Stephan (1849-1949) was born to German immigrants in Dayton, Ohio. His father left the family to join the California "Gold Rush." His mother moved to Cincinnati where young Sol was bound out to work with a pork packer. Sol Stephan had a lifelong interest in animals. As a child he kept a variety of wildlife pets. He began his professional career working with animals during the Civil War when he became a cowhand at the age of thirteen, herding cattle on the prairies of northern Indiana. Later he worked for a number of years for several circuses, where he became an elephant trainer or "bullman." Stephan's older brother, Tom, was also a circus animal trainer, specializing in big cats. Sol Stephan later described his brother as one of the best trainers in the country. Sol Stephan was six feet tall with a powerful, robust physique. He was described by a newspaper as having "ruddy cheeks" and "snapping blue eyes." Stephan had a genial manner and was a renowned story-teller.

In the late nineteenth century the boards of directors of most American zoos and other comparable institutions took a more active role in institutional operations and decision-making than today. At the Cincinnati Zoo after 1885 the Superintendent and the Secretary of the Board of Directors shared the responsibility of managing the Zoo under the direction of the Board. The Superintendent managed the animal collection and general operations, but purchases and policy decisions had to be approved by the Board. The Secretary meanwhile managed the Zoo's business, marketing, and entertainment operations.

Superintendent Sol Stephan and giraffe. Stephan started as a keeper and elephant handler in 1875. He was appointed Superintendent in 1886 and directed Zoo operations until his retirement in 1937, at the age of 88.

New Faces

The Zoo purchased two young chimpanzees in 1888, apparently the only ones in the country. The two animals fascinated visitors with their antics and gymnastic skills and were described as being always in motion and never still. The lively animals were humorously named "Mr. and Mrs. Rooney" after a couple of well-known actors. Sol Stephan trained them to eat at a table with fork and spoon, to the visitors' delight. Their cage in the Carnivora House was surrounded with a glass partition to protect them from drafts and disease.

In the early 1880s the Zoo's animal collection was boosted by bargains at auctions of bankrupt menageries. Later some of the more significant animal acquisitions included the first African hunting dogs exhibited in the United States, a young Nile hippopotamus, a manatee, two Gila monsters, tapirs, a black-footed ferret, and a whooping crane. In 1880 four passenger pigeons were hatched as well as a trumpeter swan, the first hatching of this species at a U.S. zoo. In 1882 a bison was born, one of the first to be born in captivity in North America. Other births in the 1880s included a jaguar, a grizzly bear, and more sea lions. In 1889 two polar bears were born but did not survive. In 1880 surplus prairie dogs were sent to Chicago's Lincoln Park Zoological Garden. Its superintendent and a park commissioner also came to Cincinnati to learn about sea lion care. Throughout the decade the Zoo's pair of giraffes was among the most popular of the Zoo's animals. In 1889 a baby giraffe was born, the first in America. The mother did not nurse it, however, and the baby died five days later.

A BABY GIRAFFE.

The First Born in America.

A Notable Event at the Zoological Gardens.

The Female Giraffe Successfully Delivered.

A Touching Scene Between the Mother and Her Offspring.

The Male Looks On, and Tenderly Kisses His Mate.

FEEDING THE BABY GIRAFFE.
[From an Instantaneous Photograph Taken For THE ENQUIRER.]

The Cincinnati Enquirer, 1889

Trumpeter Swans. In 1880 the Zoo hatched its first trumpeter swan which was the first hatching in an American zoo. This rare North American species is the largest of the swans.

"Mr. and Mrs. Rooney." In 1888 they were evidently the only chimpanzees in the United States. The Rooneys were named for the resemblance of the male to a famous actor of the day who dressed extravagantly for his comedy parts. The chimps were likewise dressed up for this special photograph. The renowned actor, Pat Rooney, once visited the Zoo to see his namesake. *"As he [the actor] stood before the cage with a party of friends the male chimpanzee thrust his face between the bars and pursed out his lips in a peculiarly comical manner. The actor roared with laughter, and throwing up his hands, shouted in his richest stage brogue, 'Howly smoke, but isn't he loike me?'"*

Grand Bandstand. The Cincinnati Zoo followed the nineteenth-century German zoo tradition of offering band concerts. This large bandstand was built in 1889. The fountain in the foreground was donated by Board President A. E. Burkhardt, a German-born businessman and son-in-law of Zoo founder Andrew Erkenbrecher.

ENTRANCE AND CARRIAGE STANDS.

Zoo entrance, carriage stands, and horse-drawn streetcars (lithograph from an 1880s souvenir album). By the late 1880s a narrow-gauge railroad and cable cars reached the Zoo, improving transportation.

Music at the Zoo

In 1880 a spectacular performance of "Scenes in Venice," was staged with a cast of hundreds and an enormous canvas back drop, that was painted by noted artists Henry Farny and John Rettig, recreating Saint Mark's Square. The same year a production of "Carnival Lights" used the newly-invented technology of electric lights. In 1879 and 1885 Gilbert and Sullivan's light opera, *Pinafore*, was performed utilizing the Zoo's lake. The original small bandstand was torn down in 1881. Later in 1889 a grand Moorish-styled bandstand was constructed, designed by local architect Gustav W. Drach. More elaborate concerts were performed at the Zoo on summer evenings and Sunday afternoons. The city's many German singing societies were also popular attractions for several decades.

Improvements
In Transportation

Improvements in urban transportation were critical in the development of zoos in the late 19th century. In Cincinnati transportation was especially important because its urban center is surrounded by steep hills. The hills limited both the growth of the city and easy access to outlying places like the Zoo, which was a relatively distant three miles from downtown. In the 1870s and 1880s advances in transportation, including steam-powered cable cars and inclines (inclined railroads), were introduced. By 1887 a narrow-gauge railroad was extended to the Zoo. At the Zoo entrance a broad plaza, modeled after the entrance of the Berlin Zoological Garden, was constructed to receive cable cars and their passengers. The cable car fare was only five cents compared with the ten cents that horse-drawn streetcars charged and service was twice as fast. Superintendent Sol Stephan later recalled, however, that the cable car line often ran into mechanical problems that could require hours to repair. Often these breakdowns would occur on a holiday, leaving crowds of grumbling and disgruntled passengers waiting to go home.

Financial Ups and Downs

The Zoo struggled through its early years with indebtedness from construction costs and annual rental payments. In 1881 the Annual Report gloomily announced a "... falling off in receipts from all sources. We need not go far to discover the causes of the deficiency. Last winter was long and cold, and the spring was wet and late, while the summer was unprecedented for long continued hot weather." The next year a smallpox epidemic in Cincinnati kept out-of-town visitors away, reducing attendance an estimated 10 per cent. Another financial panic struck the country in May 1884 which reduced visitor attendance from outside the city. In 1885 brewer John Hauck lent the Zoo $135,000 at a low interest rate and gained title to the property. This lessened the financial crisis and allowed the Zoo to lease the property perpetually, with the option to sell any unneeded portions. In 1886 the Board proposed that a new non-profit organization be formed, similar to Music Hall and the Cincinnati Art Museum, if the Society's stockholders would agree to relinquish their rights to dividends and the citizens of Cincinnati would contribute $60,000 to pay off existing debts. Unfortunately, many stockholders refused to give up rights to dividends and so the reorganization plan fell through. Therefore the Zoo under Board President A. E. Burkhardt, son-in-law of Zoo founder Andrew Erkenbrecher, sold 21 acres to a housing development syndicate for $90,000 in 1886. This enabled the Zoo to pay some of its debts and to add needed improvements. New exhibits, designed by architect Gustav W. Drach, were built for buffalo, wolves, prairie dogs, and birds of prey. In 1888 the Annual Report announced a financial net profit of $19,000, with receipts which "... demonstrate beyond a doubt the future success of the Zoo...." By this time Cincinnati's workers were often given a half-day off on Saturday, allowing more time for recreation and visits to the Zoo. In 1889 the Zoo deepened its relationship with the city of Cincinnati when it was incorporated into the expanding city.

The Eagle House was ninety feet long with a central dome forty-five feet high. It was among the largest free-flight exhibits in the world. Constructed in 1887, it was designed by local architect Gustav W. Drach.

Elk Park. A herd of elk or wapiti with the Zoo entrance in the background.

Carnivora House. Built in 1875, this was the largest of the Zoo's animal exhibit buildings.

The Restaurant or Clubhouse. The Clubhouse was the largest of the Zoo's buildings and served as an important civic gathering place for many decades. At the turn of the century noted local architects Samuel Hannaford & Sons designed a two-story colonnaded veranda to surround the original building. (Courtesy of Paul W. Schuch)

End of the Century: The 1890s

The sale of Zoo property in 1887 and financing through John Hauck and Julius Dexter provided economic security for the Zoo into the early 1890s. The Annual Report for 1890 boasted, "We have the largest and most complete zoological gardens in the country..." but noted "...ours is the only institution of its kind that has neither state nor municipal assistance." The Annual Report of 1891 described that year as "a season of success unprecedented in the preceding seventeen years of the Society's existence." It was estimated that two-thirds of the attendance was from outside the city limits. In 1893 the Zoo's Secretary, Charles McLean, reported that the Zoo under Board President A. E. Burkhardt "... set to work to vigorously stimulate attendance; for experience had taught that, no matter how great the (animal) collection, something more than the menagerie alone was necessary to keep the public interested. Many

and novel entertainments were given; summer night musical fetes were established. They soon became the most popular and fashionable affairs of the summer season." Musical events in 1892 included concerts by military bands, the Cincinnati Orchestra's string orchestra, and even concerts by the Royal Bell Ringers of London. Other entertainment that was offered included theater, fireworks, a roller coaster, and occasional exhibitions by acrobats, aerialists, and other performers. The Cincinnati Zoo often referred to itself by the term "resort," reflecting the growing importance of recreation and entertainment to urban society. The Zoo, located on breezy hillsides north of downtown, was a welcome refuge for city dwellers wishing to escape Cincinnati's ever-present haze of coal smoke, poor sanitation systems, and streets profusely littered with horse manure.

Musical concerts at the Zoo were stylish affairs. Cincinnati society relaxed on summer evenings among the gardens, gaslights, and music.

Early Lessons in Animal Management

Many new techniques in animal handling and management were developed in zoos during the 19th century. In this remarkable period of scientific advancement and technological innovation, a great deal was learned about zoology, animal behavior, and animal care. The experience of European zoos, as well as circuses, provided much information. Sol Stephan used his experience from circuses and from his earlier cowhand days. Stephan was an admirer of German animal handling. He frequently hired German immigrants because they were often hard-working, efficient employees and liked animals.

As one of the oldest and largest zoos in the country, the Cincinnati Zoological Garden became a model for newer zoos in other cities. In 1890 Dr. Frank Baker, then Acting Manager and later a long-time Superintendent of the new National Zoo in Washington, D.C., visited the Cincinnati Zoo and studied its operations. He reported: "I was greatly impressed with the excellent management of the gardens, which was testified by the cleanliness and order of everything and the excellent condition of the animals." Baker noted that the Cincinnati Zoo had six keepers and one night watchman who also did all the cooking for the animals. They were each paid $50 a month. Superintendent Sol Stephan was in charge of "all matters within the grounds," while advertising and arrangements for activities like music, dancing, and parties were made by the Board of Directors.

The Animal Collection

By 1895 Cincinnati's animal collection had grown to 1163 specimens: 385 mammals, 732 birds, 46 reptiles. The Winter Quarters building was constructed in 1895 to provide improved winter facilities for elephants and other warm-climate species. The Zoo and Sol Stephan were known for successful animal breeding, including grizzly bears, lions, tigers, hyenas, a kangaroo, a jaguar, and many others. In 1901 Stephan reported that he sold animals bred at the Zoo for an average of $4,000 annually. This money was used to buy new animals. He enjoyed finding rare species, the best specimens, and the best deals. When asked how he acquired outstanding animal specimens Stephan replied, "Tradin' 'round. Watchin' the dealers. You got to keep your eyes open in this business. That's the secret of getting good stock." This was how Sol Stephan built up the animal collection and the Cincinnati Zoo.

Illustration in the Zoo's 1893 guidebook.

Capturing large animals was difficult in the old days (1898). Hoofed animals that might charge were lassoed with four ropes, one in front, one behind, and one on each side with two men on each rope. Then the animal could not charge in any direction. This cowboy technique was called "walking Spanish."

Restraining a leopard. *Superintendent Sol Stephan stands to the right of the leopard. Zookeepers pull ropes attached to a board that forces the animal up against the cage bars so that it can safely be given medical treatment (1898).*

The Bear Pits.

Conserving Americana

By the early 1890s the American frontier was settled. The rapid disappearance of the nation's wildlife such as the bison and passenger pigeon initiated concerted conservation efforts to preserve natural resources and wildlife and to establish national parks and forests. Large new zoological parks at Washington, D.C., and New York were founded in part because of these concerns. At the older Cincinnati Zoological Garden, Sol Stephan made special efforts to breed then rare native mammals like bison, elk or wapiti, cougar, and grizzly bear. The Cincinnati Zoo was apparently the first zoo to breed Eastern blue jays and even had some limited success breeding passenger pigeons.

This period was accompanied by a general mood of patriotic nationalism. In the 1893 Zoo guidebook the author and Zoo Secretary, Charles McLean, argued that the grizzly bear deserved the title "King of the Beasts" rather than the lion, "... if it means to be first of the brute kind in courage, strength, and ferocity." He concluded patriotically, "The Grizzly is strictly an American institution, and of course we have the greatest of everything in America, even the monarch of the brutes." He also claimed that the Zoo's male grizzly and polar bears were the largest specimens ever known in captivity. In 1893 a bald eagle was donated to the Zoo by Ohio Governor and later President William McKinley.

The nationalistic interest in America extended beyond animals to Indians or Native Americans. In 1895 the Zoo hosted a small band of Cree for two months, followed the next year by a much larger number of Sicangu Sioux. Earlier, zoos in Europe had held similar ethnographic exhibitions. Eighty-nine Sioux from the Rosebud Reservation in South Dakota camped at the Zoo for three months.

Bison or buffalo. The Zoo's small herd of bison grew through successful breeding. The half-timbered exhibit building was constructed in 1887, designed by architect Gustav W. Drach. It was located near today's Nocturnal House. (Courtesy of the Lloyd Library and Museum)

They set up tepees, demonstrated their tribal life-styles, gave daily horseback exhibitions, and staged spectacular "Wild West" shows, reenacting stagecoach attacks, the massacre of Wounded Knee, and the battle of Little Big Horn. Although the event was expected to be a great financial success, it rained most of that summer and attendance was low. Consistent with its scientific objectives, the Zoo's 1896 Annual Board Report consoled itself that at least the event "...gave a rare opportunity of showing the character and mode of life of the Indian tribes."

Sicangu Sioux. In 1896 the Zoo hosted a large band of Sicangu Sioux who camped at the Zoo for three months. They demonstrated their tribal life-style and gave daily horseback exhibitions. (Courtesy of the Cincinnati Natural History Museum)

Zoo Education

Education continued to be an important mission of the Cincinnati Zoological Garden. In 1893 the Zoo published an informative, illustrated guidebook, "A Book about the Zoo." In addition to labeling its animal exhibits, Superintendent Sol Stephan had many of the trees labeled in 1894 through the efforts of botanist Dr. Albert Leue.

Although children have always been attracted to the Zoo and its animals, in the 1890s the Zoo developed a new relationship with public school education. In 1896 the Cincinnati public schools began a policy of sending tens of thousands of school children to the Zoo twice each school year to study the animals. According to a later book about Cincinnati, the Zoo was "... for many years an educational agency whose value it would be impossible to estimate too highly."

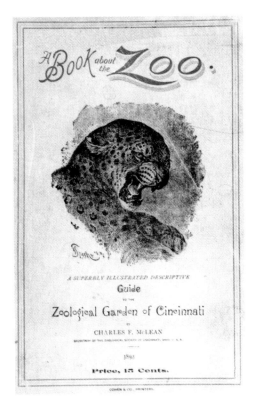

Zoo guidebook. An informative illustrated guidebook was published in 1893.

Children at the Sea Lion Pool. *Children have always been especially fascinated by animals, particularly active, intelligent species like California sea lions. (Courtesy of The Cincinnati Historical Society)*

Ups and Downs

After several successful years in the early 1890s, another major financial panic or crash struck in 1893 with dire effects on the Cincinnati Zoo. According to Sol Stephan, the keepers and other employees were not paid for several months. Stephan occasionally gave them money out of his own pocket. One day the Board of Directors announced to Stephan that they had decided to sell the Zoo and its animals. Stephan called his employees together and said to them, " 'Boys, I have a few hundred dollars saved up. I want you to stick with me through the winter. I can't give you a regular wage at this time but whenever you need five or ten dollars come and see me. By spring I am confident everything will be all right.' The employees, to a man, pledged to stick with him. Stephan then went to the Board and told them what the men had decided." Later a Board member, John Goetz, Jr., told Stephan that, "...he had raised $10,000 to see the Zoo through the winter. He was prompted to do this, he said, by the sacrifice the men were making to keep the Zoo going and by Stephan's confidence in the future."

Asian elephant with trainer Ed Coyne and visitors. Ed Coyne started working at the Zoo as a boy at the age of ten in 1877. His father was a zookeeper, who suddenly died on the job. Young Eddie was given a part-time job at the pony track. Later as a young man he became a fulltime keeper. He was one of the Zoo's leading keepers for 65 years, working until 1942 when he died at the age of 75. (Courtesy of The Cincinnati Historical Society)

HIS MAJESTY OF BENGAL.

Bengal Tiger. Many of the often dramatic illustrations in the Zoo's 1893 guidebook were masterfully crafted by the well-known artist Friedrich Specht of Berlin, Germany.

The Zoo Entrance. Women and their young children have always been among the most frequent of zoo visitors.

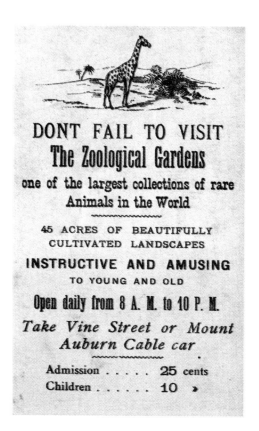

Advertising card from the 1890s.

Going to the Zoo

By the end of the century much of Cincinnati's population had moved away from downtown to the surrounding suburbs and hillsides. The lack of accessible metropolitan transportation was a major cause of the financial problems that beset the 19th-century Cincinnati Zoo, in addition to periodic business depressions. Board reports complained about the poor transit facilities which were expensive to construct because of the city's hilly topography. Zoo officials believed that if the transit facilities had been adequate, receipts could easily have been 50% higher. At the end of the century different competing streetcar company lines were merged under one company, which allowed inexpensive transfers. In comparison, by 1891 the Philadelphia Zoological Garden had much better urban transportation. The Philadelphia Zoo was located on rent-free municipal land while in the late 1880s and 1890s the Cincinnati Zoo had to pay over $8,000 a year in rent, taxes, and interest (equivalent to $125,000 today). Attendance at the Cincinnati Zoo in 1896 rose to 271,080, up from 222,492 in 1891. Many of the visitors were German-Americans. They were especially noticeable on concert days and summer festivals. After 1896 a "German Day" event was held on the first Sunday in September, annually attracting over 10,000 people with singing, picnics, speeches, and camaraderie.

After struggling with the effects of the financial panic of 1893 and a resulting depression, the Zoological Society went into receivership in 1898. The receivers were mayor of Cincinnati Gustav Tafel, a former Zoo Board President, and George Hafer, a former Board member. The receivers blamed the financial failure on the expense of the Zoo's "outside attractions," including the costly music performances, ethnographic displays, and other events.

The Zoological Society never made any financial profits. After the Cincinnati Zoo's early years many of its investors evidently gave up hope of financial gain, and supported the Zoo for its civic benefits to the community. Likewise, most of the European for-profit zoos, which the Cincinnati Zoological Garden was modeled after, were not successful financial ventures. Generally, any profits that these zoos made were reinvested back into the institutions. By 1920 most of these European zoos had changed to a nonprofit status.

A city-wide movement to preserve the Cincinnati Zoo was organized by Albert Fischer, an original founder and business associate of Andrew Erkenbrecher. In 1899 Cincinnati voters approved purchasing the Zoological Garden, but the city never exercised the authority. A host of civic-minded benefactors stepped forward to pay off the debts with banker and original Zoo stockholder L. B. Harrison playing a key role. Many of the creditors generously helped by being lenient in their claims. Later in 1899 a corporation, the Cincinnati Zoological Company, was established to operate the Cincinnati Zoological Garden on a nonprofit basis.

At the end of the century German animal dealer and zoo authority Carl Hagenbeck visited all of the major zoos of the world. He noted that none were superior to the Cincinnati Zoo in many respects, in spite of its precarious financial status. Hagenbeck especially commended the care and condition of the Zoo's animal collection as well as its buildings and grounds.

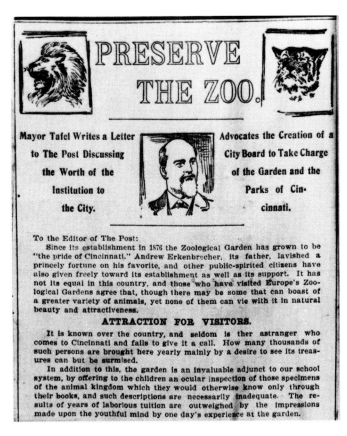

Newspaper letter to the editor from Mayor Gustav Tafel, who was a former President of the Zoo's Board of Directors. (Courtesy of the Cincinnati Post)

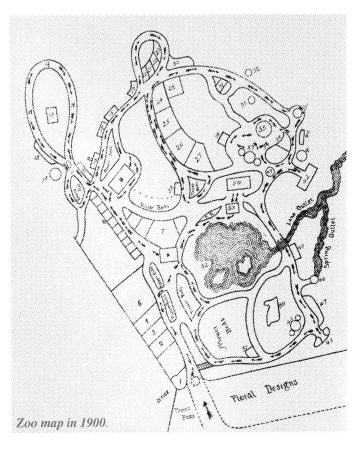

Zoo map in 1900.

LOCATION OF ALL BUILDINGS AND ANIMALS.
Arrows show Route to be taken. Cincinnati Zoological Garden.

1 Main Entrance	21 Ostrich Inclosure	39 Mink
2 Llama	22 Emu Inclosure	40 First Cage of the Zoo
3 Black Fallow Deer	23 Hog Deer Inclosure	41 Alligator Basin
4 Siberian Camel	24 Spotted Axis Deer In-	42 Winter Quarters and
5 Elk	closure	Pavillion
6 Monkey House	25 Camel Yard	43 Coon Tree
7 Pheasant Yard	26 Zebra Yard	44 Carp Pond and Water
8 Avaries	27 Mountain Goats and	Fall
9 Carnivora Building	Sheep	45 Zebu Yard
10 Carousel	28 Snake Cage	46 Spring
11 Squirrel House	29 White Fallow Deer	47 Virginia Deer
12 Amphitheatre	30 Red Deer	48 Small Animal House
13 Elephant and Camel	31 Bear Pits	49 Eagle and Vulture
Stand	32 Small Fox House	House
14 Pony Race Track	33 Small Skunk House	50 Proposed Elephant
15 Green House	34 Badger Cage	House
16 Generating Station	35 Sea Lion Basin	51 Owl Cage
17 Yak Inclosure	36 Water Buffalo	52 Lake
18 Buffalo Inclosure	37 Proposed Lilly and	53 Band Stand
19 Wolf Dens	Fish Ponds	54 Restaurant
20 Kangaroo	38 Prairie Dogs	

A young male tiger. A photograph by noted photographer Enno Meyer, who took many animal photos for the Zoo during the early 1900s.

Electric Trolley. For many years visitors traveled to the Zoo by trolleys or streetcars. (Courtesy of The Cincinnati Historical Society)

New Era: 1900-1916

American workers at the turn of the century had a shorter work week than previously with more recreational time for themselves and their families. In large cities transit companies often built amusement and entertainment facilities as attractive destinations to encourage more weekend trolley business. In the early part of 1902 the Cincinnati Traction Company, which had just bought all of its competitors' lines, purchased controlling shares of stock in the Cincinnati Zoological Company, although later in the year it unsuccessfully tried to give the Zoo to the city. In addition to an altruistic desire to help the Zoological Garden, the Traction Company also undoubtedly intended to benefit from increased rider traffic, especially on weekends. A new Board of Directors was elected with the Traction Company's President W. Kesley Schoepf

selected as President. A program of improvements was adopted and with the Traction Company's support the Zoo finally received easily accessible public transportation.

During this period the Zoo was operated on a nonprofit basis. It was a successful time for the Zoo. New buildings, exhibits, and improvements were added. The animal collection grew and the grounds became filled with flower beds. Twelve acres were purchased, increasing the size of the Zoo to 57 acres. Throughout the era annual paid attendance varied from 240,000 to 360,000. The Zoo was an important regional tourist destination. It was still the largest zoo in the Midwest and the only major zoo within 250 miles of Cincinnati.

Huge Pythons were sensational attractions in the early 1900s. One of the Zoo's pythons was 25 feet long.

Buffalo Range, Zoological Gardens, Cincinnati, Ohio.

Bison at the "Buffalo Range." In 1903 the Cincinnati Zoo built a three-acre exhibit for the then almost extinct bison or buffalo. The Zoo's herd was one of the two largest bison herds in American zoos.

New Exhibits

Before the turn of the century new zoos in Washington, D.C., and New York began to exhibit herds of bison, deer, and other hoofed animals in larger, more natural, fenced exhibits. These new zoos were more spacious than earlier zoological gardens, from 180 to 270 acres in size compared to Cincinnati's then 57 acres. Because of their larger size and their wilder, more natural landscape, these new institutions called themselves zoological parks in order to distinguish themselves from the earlier zoological gardens. To the public, however, both zoological parks and zoological gardens became popularly known simply as "zoos."

At this time there was a widespread interest by American zoos in preserving and exhibiting native species of animals like bison whose populations had recently dramatically decreased. In late 1902 Zoo Superintendent Sol Stephan visited the new eastern zoological parks and returned with ideas for two new exhibits in Cincinnati. In 1903 a spacious three-acre exhibit was opened, called the "Buffalo Range," for the then almost extinct bison or buffalo. The Zoo had one of the largest bison herds among American zoos.

"Bismark, Zoological Gardens, Cincinnati, O."

"Bismark", a male bison or buffalo, described as the largest bison in captivity. (Courtesy of Pamela S. Brown)

The Elephant House, originally called the Herbivora Building, opened in 1906. Sited on the Zoo's highest point, it was designed as a dramatic spectacle which could be seen at a distance by visitors approaching on the Vine Street trolley line. This grand monument, which cost the then extravagant sum of $50,000, was one of the largest zoo buildings in the world (150' long x 75' high x 75' wide), with advanced animal quarters especially designed to facilitate breeding. The noted local architectural firm of Elzner & Anderson modeled their design of the building after a variety of Islamic architectural influences, including India's Taj Mahal. Alfred O. Elzner had earlier studied under Henry Hobson Richardson, one of America's premier architects, while George M. Anderson had attended the prestigious École des Beaux Arts in Paris. In 1903 their firm had designed America's first reinforced concrete skyscraper, the Ingalls Building, which was built in downtown Cincinnati. At the time, the construction of the Elephant House's towering curved domes was undoubtedly a difficult architectural challenge that was solved through Elzner & Anderson's concrete construction technology.

In the latter part of the 19th century, zoo architecture utilized foreign or vernacular architectural forms to express the exotic origins of exhibited animals. The Cincinnati Zoo's Elephant House and other similar zoo buildings in Europe, particularly those at the Berlin Zoological Garden, were among the last and most spectacular examples of this early style of zoo architecture. At this time other American zoos, led by the New York Zoological Park (or the "Bronx Zoo"), were turning to neo-classical architectural styles. Soon, however, a radically different kind of zoo architecture with barless, outdoor exhibits would develop in Europe that would, like the Cincinnati Zoo's Elephant House, use a new technology of concrete construction.

In 1902 the Zoo, under its new Board of Directors, bought an expensive carousel from Gustav Dentzel, one of the nation's leading manufacturers, located in Philadelphia. The carousel or merry-go-round was seventy feet in diameter and described as the finest in the country. The new attraction cost $11,000, and in addition Dentzel required that the Zoo build a $4,000 building, specially designed to protect the ride from the elements. It remained at the Zoo until it was sold in 1974.

In 1912 Cincinnati's oldest surviving building, the Kemper Log House, was moved to the Zoo as a civic historical exhibit. Originally built in 1804, it remained at the Zoo until 1981 when it was moved to Sharon Woods Village.

The Elephant House or Herbivora Building opened in 1906. This monumental building cost the then extravagant sum of $50,000. Today it is one of the most spectacular historic buildings in the zoo world and is listed on the National Register of Historic Places. (Courtesy of Chuck Bricking)

Advertisement. Sol Stephan, the Cincinnati Zoo's Superintendent, was Carl Hagenbeck's representative in North America. (From The Barnum & Bailey Annual Route Book and Illustrated Tours, 1906)

Hagenbeck's Tierpark in Hamburg, Germany, opened in 1907 and featured spectacular barless exhibits. (Courtesy of Carl Hagenbeck's Tierpark)

Carl Hagenbeck and His Influence

In the early years of the twentieth century entrepreneur and showman Carl Hagenbeck (1844-1913) of Hamburg, Germany, revolutionized the design of zoos by creating new barless animal exhibits. The world's leading animal dealer, he also developed and popularized many innovations in animal management. He was the first to demonstrate that many of the larger tropical mammals and birds could become acclimated to the winter weather of temperate climate zoos. Hagenbeck was also famous for his use of kindness in training and handling animals.

There was a general trend toward greater naturalism in zoos through the 19th century. In America the new zoological parks in Washington, D.C., and New York brought increased spaciousness and a more natural landscape to zoo design. Hagenbeck went even further with radical advances in zoo design. He eliminated bars, cages, and fencing for many animals and used instead a new technology of artificial rockwork and moats. Conventional architecture was replaced with artificial mountains and rock outcrops. The result was a more naturalistic and less architectural zoo. Hagenbeck's barless exhibits were also visually spectacular and dramatic, giving zoo visitors new interest and excitement. The world's first barless exhibits opened in 1907 at his animal park (Tierpark) near Hamburg. The Tierpark attracted international attention in the zoo world and visiting celebrities from European royalty to American inventor Thomas Edison.

For many years Carl Hagenbeck was the world's largest animal dealer, with a worldwide network of agents and collectors. In America the Cincinnati Zoo's Secretary, Lee Williams, was Hagenbeck's representative for several years. In 1902 Superintendent Sol Stephan became the Hagenbeck representative. The Zoo evidently benefited from this arrangement because Hagenbeck animals for sale were displayed at the Zoo without cost to the Zoo. When Hagenbeck shipped animals to Stephan he provided information on care and feeding. Both Stephan and Hagenbeck were known for their skill in handling animals. The two became good friends as did Stephan's son, Joe, and the Hagenbeck sons, Heinrich and Lorenz. When the Hagenbecks visited Cincinnati on business they often stayed with the Stephans. The families were so close that Lorenz called Sol Stephan "my American father."

During the early 1900s the touring Hagenbeck animal show gave performances at the Cincinnati Zoo during the summer season. The winter quarters of the Hagenbeck American circus were located only five miles north of the Zoo at the Carthage Fairgrounds. Lorenz Hagenbeck, the youngest Hagenbeck son, managed the circus.

After the 1905 summer circus season, Lorenz Hagenbeck brought Sol Stephan's son, Joe, back to Hamburg, Germany, with him. Joe Stephan was assisting his father at the Cincinnati Zoo and was a veterinary student. In Germany young Stephan lived with the Hagenbecks, learned techniques of animal management, and worked on the construction of their revolutionary new barless zoo. He also visited a number of European zoos with Lorenz Hagenbeck. In January 1906 Joe Stephan traveled with Lorenz Hagenbeck on an expedition to ship 2,000 camels for the German government. The camels were purchased at exotic ports along the Red Sea, shipped down the African coast, and around the Cape of Good Hope to German South West Africa. It was one of the largest animal shipments that the Hagenbeck firm ever undertook and it was filled with adventures for Joe Stephan.

Sol Stephan was among the earliest American advocates of the Hagenbeck barless exhibits. He said that they were cheaper than conventional exhibit buildings, more educational, and more attractive. In addition the animals were happier in them than in small bare cages. In 1913 Sol Stephan predicted that it was "only a question of time" before zoos of the future would become barless and cageless.

Hagenbeck's new zoo under construction with Joe Stephan (left) and Lorenz Hagenbeck (right) in the foreground.

Joe Stephan feeding the Hagenbecks' black-footed penguins. Stephan learned the Hagenbecks' animal management practices in Hamburg, Germany.

The Hagenbeck zebra carriage in Hamburg, Germany. Heinrich Hagenbeck is driving while Joe Stephan, Carl Hagenbeck, and his wife are passengers.

An American Zoo Pioneer

By 1900 Sol Stephan had directed Cincinnati Zoo operations for fourteen years. He had 25 years of zoo experience with several years of circus background. According to the *Illustrated Buffalo (N.Y.) Express* (Dec. 29, 1901), he was regarded as "the leading expert in America on animals and zoos, and recognized as one of the greatest authorities in the world." Stephan was not an academic zoologist. He had little formal education. He was a professional "zoo man" with a wide range of experience managing animals and a lot of common sense. He spoke in an informal, folksy manner with what was described by the *Cleveland Plain Dealer* as a plainsman's accent. During his career Sol Stephan edited several of the Cincinnati Zoo guide books, including the informative "Studies in Zoology," published in 1900.

Sol Stephan, General Manager of the Zoo, was an early advocate of the barless, naturalistic exhibits which Carl Hagenbeck developed.

"Brutus," a magnificent male lion. Sol Stephan loved many of the large felines. As he walked through the Carnivora House he would stop at each cage " ...to have a little chat with the big cats...the lions rubbed themselves against the bars so ecstatically that they almost played a tune on them." (Courtesy of Pamela S. Brown)

Sol Stephan loved animals and was an advocate of kindness in handling and training. He encouraged keepers to talk to their animals in a friendly tone to establish a good relationship. According to the *Cincinnati Times-Star*, as he walked through the Carnivora House Sol would stop at each cage "... to have a little chat with the big cats. The leopards purred and rolled over and over on the floor; the tigers stretched themselves on their backs and made playful stabs at the air with their paws, all the time looking sidewise out of their yellow eyes at Sol; the lions rubbed themselves against the bars so ecstatically that they almost played a tune on them."

Sol Stephan placed great importance on animal diets. Fresh grass was fed to many herbivores along with leafy branches of trees and shrubs. Sugar beets grown on the grounds were a great favorite of many herbivores. Oat seedlings were grown in the greenhouse during the winter for many of the birds. Horsemeat was fed to most of the carnivores while the more valuable big cats dined on beef.

Stephan was renowned for his skills in animal breeding. As early as 1901 he advocated that zoos should exchange individual animals for breeding to broaden bloodlines and increase the genetic diversity of captive populations. Stephan told Buffalo Zoological Garden officials, "The more zoos, the better. It means an exchange of animals. It means less inbreeding; in fact, no inbreeding. In your present zoo you have animals that have been inbred. We have an elk in our zoo that would make two of the elk in your zoo. Animals could be exchanged and there would be an end to inbred, small, inferior animals. Take a buffalo herd, for instance. After a few years zoos could exchange bulls for a time. Just so, they could exchange other animals and you will see that the more zoos there are the finer the animals will be."

Sol Stephan's skills in animal breeding were featured in this newspaper cartoon.

Ostriches in the snow with Hagenbeck's Tierpark under construction in the background. Carl Hagenbeck discovered that many larger tropical animals readily acclimate to the colder weather of temperate climates. Sol Stephan was an early advocate of this practice which is used today in temperate climate zoos throughout the world.

Sol Stephan was a noted storyteller with a dry wit. He was popular with employees, Board members, donors, and other zoo officials. Stephan loved children. A woman who was a little girl in the early 1900s recently remembered him as someone whom children "liked to be around." She said that he was "the most delightful man going," adding, "I loved him like I loved my father."

Sol Stephan was a good friend of other zoo directors and officials and was often consulted about zoo and animal management. Stephan's office at the Zoo entrance was later described by Lorenz Hagenbeck as "a great meeting-place for American zoo owner-proprietors, who were always glad to discuss business with the old man and do business with him too." Stephan was undoubtedly an important information channel between the Hagenbecks with their contacts at European zoos and the early American zoos. He appears to have been an important part of a "good old boy" network of zoo officials, which existed in the days before the American Association of Zoological Parks and Aquariums was formed in 1924 as a part of the American Institute of Park Executives.

Sol Stephan was called the "Boss" by his respectful employees. He had a commanding presence and paid keen attention to details. The *Cleveland Plain Dealer* reported, "Everything neat and clean and recently painted. Alertness was in the atmosphere of the Cincinnati Zoo." It continued, "He's relentless for maintenance. Let a buck rip a strand of wire in a fence and he has it repaired immediately. Let a rail on the pony track fence come loose and he has it nailed back before you can say Jack Robinson." "The animals and the trees aren't the only things well kept.... Everything neat and clean and recently painted.... Efficiency! Alertness! Comfort and service! Sol A. Stephan on the job and everyone under him on his toes."

Sol Stephan's title changed from Superintendent to General Manager, managing the animal collection and general operations. He shared executive responsibility with the Zoo's Secretary in cooperatively managing the Zoo. Both the General Manager and the Secretary served as officers on the Board of Directors. The Secretary managed the Zoo's business, marketing, and varied entertainment operations, and occasionally was listed as the Business Agent. In 1902 the Zoo's Secretary, Lee Williams, left to manage Carl Hagenbeck's American animal show. He was replaced by Walter A. Draper. Draper later became the President of the Cincinnati Traction Company and a prominent civic leader. He served as a key Zoo Board member for several decades and was a good friend of Sol Stephan. After 1913 the Zoo hired a Business Manager to manage its business operations.

In 1907 Sol Stephan visited the major zoological gardens of Europe for the first time. He reported that most of these older zoos were showing their age. Many were not well maintained and were becoming run down. Although some had larger animal collections, he thought that overall none were finer than the Cincinnati Zoo, because of its superior landscape, buildings, grounds, and general maintenance.

Moving a giraffe for the opening of the new Elephant House in 1906. Notice the heavily padded walls of this wagon that was pulled by six horses. (Courtesy of Pamela S. Brown)

"Rough Riding" With Teddy Roosevelt

During his administration from 1901 to 1909 President Theodore Roosevelt established major conservation programs in the United States. These created national parks and forests and greatly increased public awareness of nature and conservation. He was one of the nation's most popular presidents and was earlier a hero of the Spanish-American War, where he led his "Rough Rider" regiment to victory. As President he visited the Zoo and became acquainted with the Stephans. Young Joe Stephan, who was then 23, had a bad sinus infection. The President thought young Stephan would benefit from the drier climate at his ranch in North Dakota. He invited Joe there in 1903 for a summer of invigorating ranch life and to experience, in Roosevelt's words, "...the glory of work and the joy of living."

In 1905 the Zoo's young pair of giraffes was named "Kermit" and "Alice" after two of Roosevelt's children. Alice Roosevelt married Cincinnati Congressman Nicholas Longworth III, who later became Speaker of the House.

Bear cubs and zookeeper (from Leslie's Weekly, *August 3, 1905). During Teddy Roosevelt's presidency "teddy bears" became popular toys and symbols of a new and friendlier attitude toward wildlife.*

Joe Stephan at President Roosevelt's ranch near Medora, North Dakota. President Roosevelt invited Joe Stephan to his ranch in the summer of 1903.

"Rough riding" at President Roosevelt's ranch.

The Animal Collection

The Zoo benefited from its Hagenbeck connections, receiving a number of rare species as well as outstanding specimens of more common species. Carl Hagenbeck gave the Zoo a pair of Andean condors, one of which lived for many years. In 1911 the Zoo purchased an enormous male lion from the Hagenbecks which was supposedly the largest in captivity. Originally named "Kaiser," in Cincinnati he was patriotically renamed "Teddy" after President Roosevelt.

Sol Stephan was nationally renowned for his success in animal breeding. The notable species that were bred included a female giraffe that was born in 1910 and lived for many years. A newspaper in 1910 reported the birth of rare "black and white" lemurs, which were evidently ruffed lemurs. In 1912 baby beavers were raised, according to a newspaper, the first in captivity. In spite of the limitations of veterinary medicine at the time, a number of the Zoo's animals were renowned for having reached remarkably old ages in captivity. In 1910 the Zoo's beloved old Abyssinian ground hornbill, "Jack," died. He was almost 40 years old and was one of the Zoo's original animals. Jack had escaped on his first day at the Zoo and flew off to Burnet Woods Park but returned the next day.

The bird collection was one of Sol Stephan's favorites. He said, "You can't have too many birds.... They're easy to get and easy to keep and breed and there's nothing like 'em to attract the women and children." Other favorite animals of Sol Stephan were the big cats and elephants. "Brutus" and "Nero" were handsome male lions that were special friends. Another favorite was "Hatnee," a female Asian elephant whom Stephan considered the most gentle elephant in the country. "Lil" was another docile female elephant; purchased in 1918, she lived for many years after. In her younger days Lil was used occasionally for odd jobs around the Zoo: hauling tree trunks, pushing stalled vehicles, pulling up old fire hydrants, as well as giving rides to children.

Kaiser Wilhelm II, the ruler of Germany, with the Hagenbecks and the Cincinnati Zoo's baby hippo. The Kaiser, Carl Hagenbeck and his sons watch a baby hippo that was later sent to the Cincinnati Zoo. Kaiser Wilhelm II is on the left next to Carl Hagenbeck; Heinrich Hagenbeck is on the right without a hat.

Przewalski Horse. The only species of wild horse, they were first discovered in Mongolia in 1879. The Bronx Zoo ordered the first pair to be exhibited in the United States from Carl Hagenbeck. The Bronx Zoo rejected the female as a poor specimen, so Hagenbeck sent the pair to the Cincinnati Zoo in 1905. The pair and their offspring were exhibited for many years.

Since the Zoo's opening many of the deceased animals were donated to the Cincinnati Society of Natural History (today's Cincinnati Museum of Natural History), the University of Cincinnati, and the Ohio Medical College. According to the Natural History Society's 1902 guidebook, most of the mammal collection in its museum came from the Zoo. Its noted taxidermist, Charles Dury, lived near the Zoo. His studies of living animals at the Zoo gave his mounted specimens special realism.

During this era the Zoo published two educational booklets about its animals in addition to its guidebook. The first was a popular text, called "Zig Zags at the Zoo," which sold for five cents. It provided interesting information about the Zoo's animals and included a list of recommended books for further reading. The other was a twelve-page instructional manual, primarily for school teachers, called "How to Study the Animals at the Zoological Garden" by Michael F. Guyer, zoology professor at the University of Cincinnati.

Elk or wapiti with the Aviaries in the distance. (Courtesy of Pamela S. Brown)

"Hatnee," a female Asian elephant, her trainer, Ed Coyne, and admirers. (Courtesy of Pamela S. Brown)

The Last of Their Species

Passenger pigeons were once the most numerous bird species in the world. Larger than mourning doves, they lived and nested in the vast forests that covered eastern North America. The pigeons fed on a wide variety of fruits, berries, buds, seeds, and nuts, including beechnuts, acorns, and chestnuts. Their enormous flocks, which numbered in the millions, darkened the skies as they swiftly flew. According to naturalist Aldo Leopold, passenger pigeons were not merely birds, but a "biological storm." He wrote, "Yearly the feathered tempest roared up, down, and across the continent, sucking up the laden fruits of forest and prairie, burning them in a traveling blast of life." Millions of birds nested together in dense colonial sites covering acres of forests and filling the trees with nests. On the site of the Zoo passenger pigeons fed in the oak and beech trees and had even reputedly nested there.

In the late 19th century the passenger pigeon populations dropped dramatically due to the ruthless greed of commercial hunting for sales in eastern food markets and to the widespread loss of their forest habitat to agriculture and lumbering. Passenger pigeons had been exhibited at the Cincinnati Zoo since 1876 when they were described in a guidebook as "common in North America." In 1878 several pairs of birds were purchased for $2.50 a pair. By 1885 fourteen pigeons had been hatched in captive broods. After that, however, all of the Zoo's efforts to breed its passenger pigeons failed. Although the wild populations of passenger pigeons were steadily declining throughout the latter half of the 19th century, after 1890 the numbers of birds dropped dramatically. It was then clear that passenger pigeons were on the verge of extinction. After 1899 the Cincinnati Zoo had a standing offer of $1000 to buy another pair of passenger pigeons for breeding. Unfortunately, it was futile. As a last resort the Zoo even tried to breed its only remaining female, "Martha," with other species of pigeons. Martha was evidently named for Martha Washington. She was one of the Cincinnati Zoo's most popular and publicized animals in her last years. Ornithologists traveled from around the world to see her. According to Sol Stephan, she was one of the passenger pigeons hatched at the Zoo in 1885, although his accounts of her origins and age were sometimes contradictory. Martha finally died, an old and frail bird, at the reported age of 29 on September 1, 1914. Her body was packed in ice and sent to the Smithsonian Institution in Washington, D.C., where it remains today.

"Martha," the last passenger pigeon. Passenger pigeons were once the most numerous bird species on earth. Martha, the last known passenger pigeon, died September 1, 1914, at the Cincinnati Zoo.

The last captive Carolina parakeet also died at the Cincinnati Zoo, in 1918. Carolina parakeets were the only parrot species that nested in the United States. Divided by ornithologists into eastern and western subspecies or races, these small parrots were once common in the lowland forests and swamps of the eastern United States. They occasionally ranged as far north as New York and Wisconsin and as far west as Texas and Colorado. Like the passenger pigeons, Carolina parakeets were exterminated because of hunting and the destruction of forests. Unfortunately, flocks of the parakeets feasted on cultivated crops and were easily shot by farmers due to a peculiar defensive behavior of the species. When one bird in a flock was wounded, the other parakeets would often hover and call around their companion rather than fly away. Many other birds were thus easily shot. Although this behavior of the parakeets apparently often confused and intimidated small predators, against human firearms this behavior was fatal. Carolina parakeets were also captured to become popular cage birds in America and Europe. Their bright green plumage, accented by yellow-orange head feathers, was also prized for decorating women's hats. By the middle of the 19th-century the populations of Carolina parakeets were greatly reduced throughout their range.

Carolina parakeets (or parrakeets) are remembered today along with passenger pigeons at the Passenger Pigeon Memorial building.

In 1886 the Cincinnati Zoo bought a number of Carolina parakeets from Florida for $2.50 each. A number of young birds were hatched and raised at the Zoo. Generally, however, the birds were inattentive parents and often tossed their eggs out of their nests. The Carolina parakeets lived for many years at the Zoo, but gradually the individuals died. The last birds attracted a great deal of interest from zoologists and other zoos. In 1911 one of the last pairs was sent to the Bronx Zoo. Later the London Zoo offered $400 for the last pair, but the offer was refused. The last bird, a male named "Incas," died on February 21, 1918, thirty-two years after it was purchased and only months after the death of its mate, "Lady Jane." According to Sol Stephan, after Lady Jane died Incas grew increasingly listless until he finally died. There is no record of what happened to the body of Incas after his death. Both Carolina parakeets and passenger pigeons are remembered today at the Passenger Pigeon Memorial building.

The Aviaries housed many of the Zoo's birds including passenger pigeons and Carolina parakeets. In 1974 all but one of the buildings were demolished. The remaining Aviary building is preserved today as the Passenger Pigeon Memorial.

Advertising, Publicity, and Post Cards

The twentieth century brought increased commerce, advertising, and publicity to American life. Cincinnati Zoo advertising was displayed on streetcars. Newspapers highlighted human interest stories about animals as well as Zoo entertainment features. The Cincinnati Zoo was renowned throughout the country. Short movies about the Zoo were shown at theaters in the region and distributed throughout the United States, Canada, and Europe. Illustrated lectures were presented to local schools and other groups.

By 1900 workers had more leisure time for family recreation, weekend outings, and vacations. Railroads brought visitors to Cincinnati and the Zoo from towns and villages as far away as 150 miles. Parking was available at the Zoo for automobiles. After 1900 post cards became very popular in America. Memorable Cincinnati Zoo scenes and experiences were photographically reproduced for visitors to send to friends and relatives. Post cards helped to popularize the Zoo as a regional tourist attraction and destination.

Greeting from the Zoological Gardens. *Popular animals, exhibits, and Zoo scenes were favorite subjects of post cards. Black and white photographs were attractively hand tinted. (Courtesy of Pamela S. Brown)*

The Monkey House about 1905. In 1951 it was converted to the Reptile House. Originally built in 1875, it is now the oldest American zoo building. (Courtesy of Pamela S. Brown)

Giraffes, kangaroos, and zebras.

Lion, tiger, leopard, and sea lion.
(Courtesy of Pamela S. Brown)

"Zee-koe," a young hippo, was one of the most popular and one of the most valuable animals at the Zoo in the early 1900s. In 1902 he was acquired from the Hagenbeck firm of Hamburg, Germany, at a cost of $3,000. He died in 1923 after swallowing a ball. He was mounted by famed naturalist and taxidermist Carl Akeley in a display at Chicago's Field Museum of Natural History.

The Eagle House was built in 1887. It was located east of the Elephant House. It was later replaced by the present Flight Cages, built in 1970.

The Pony Track was popular with young visitors for many decades. It was located west of today's Insectarium and Nocturnal House. (Courtesy of Pamela S. Brown)

Gondolas at the Zoo. For a brief time young Zoo visitors were entertained on gondolas, apparently earlier used in a local musical performance. (Courtesy of Pamela S. Brown)

Gardens At the Zoo

14875 SCENE IN ZOOLOGICAL GARDENS, CINCINNATI, OHIO.

Gardens and trees were important features of the Zoo in the early 1900s. Many of the Zoo's trees were labeled with common and scientific names.

In the Zoo's early decades Albert Erkenbrecher, Board member and son of the founder of the Zoo, Andrew Erkenbrecher, tried to establish a botanical garden adjacent to the Zoo. He was, however, unable to obtain sufficient financing. The botanical collection and gardens were instead incorporated into the overall Zoo landscape. This was carried out with colorful flower beds, lush lawns, unusual plants, and a large number of labeled trees thought at the time to include "practically every tree that will grow in this climate." Superintendent Sol Stephan was especially fond of trees because of the shade they provided for both visitors and animals. A variety of "gardenesque"-style flower beds were added to the original park landscape and transformed the Zoo into an elegant Victorian-era stroll garden. Visitors to the Zoo of modest means could experience the kind of stately pleasure gardens that wealthy industrialists and businessmen were then creating in their lavish private estates. Head Gardener Ben Glins managed the gardens for many years. His careful eye for detail created colorful flower beds, lush manicured lawns, and closely-trimmed hedges.

14876 BAND STAND, ZOOLOGICAL GARDENS, CINCINNATI, OHIO.

Gardens and Bandstand. Colorful formal flower beds, popular at the turn of the century, combined with cultural attractions to create an elegant park setting.

The Bandstand featured afternoon and evening concerts by some of the nation's finest bands. (Courtesy of Pamela S. Brown)

Cultural Events

Band Shell. In 1911 the bandstand built in 1889 was replaced by a larger neo-classical band shell, designed by Elzner and Anderson. Here summer concerts were performed, including performances by the Cincinnati Symphony Orchestra. These facilities stood where the Gibbon Islands are located today. (Courtesy of Pamela S. Brown)

Musical performances continued at the Zoo. Some of the nation's leading bands played in popular summer afternoon and evening concerts. Later, performances by the Cincinnati Symphony Orchestra became regular features and provided summer employment for the musicians. In 1911 Board President Edward Goepper reported that "... it is not only the province of the Zoological Garden to provide music of undoubted character and highest standard, but it is also proper and natural that the people of Cincinnati should expect an opportunity of hearing the best music at the Zoo." That year a new, much larger band or orchestra shell replaced the bandstand built in 1889. The Cincinnati Symphony Orchestra's noted conductor, Leopold Stokowski, made suggestions in the planning of the new Beaux Arts-style band shell, designed by architects Elzner & Anderson.

During the summer Shakespearean plays were performed by the Ben Greet Players, a leading theatrical company. These and other entertainment were staged at the Woodland Theater. This outdoor facility was located northeast of Swan Lake, where the Botanical Center and Education Center stand today.

Nile hippopotamus. In the early years of the twentieth century the Zoo's popular hippos produced several babies.

Change In Owners: 1917-1932

After 1909 the Zoo suffered growing annual deficits. Among the competitors for visitors were movie theaters and various amusement parks. After the recession of 1913-1914 the Cincinnati Traction Company, the Zoo's major stockholder, could no longer afford to support the Zoo. It was itself strained by increasing competition from automobiles. A large-scale civic campaign was organized to save the Zoo involving the mayor, a citizens' committee chaired by August Herrmann, and a ladies' auxiliary committee. The result was an offer in the fall of 1916 by prominent local philanthropists Mrs. Anna Sinton Taft and Mrs. Mary M. Emery to contribute $250,000 if the public would raise an additional $125,000. The Traction Company then lowered the price to $250,000 allowing the $125,000, contributed by the public, to be used for needed improvements. Mrs. Taft and Mrs. Emery offered to pay for any deficits for five years and later extended this offer.

The new Cincinnati Zoological Park Association was organized as a nonprofit corporation on May 1, 1917. Mrs. Taft's husband, Charles Phelps Taft, became the President of the new Board of Directors, serving until his death in 1929. Taft, a newspaper publisher and the older half-brother of President William Howard Taft, was one of the original members of the Board of Directors.

Charles G. Miller was named the Secretary and Business Manager of the new corporation. Described as a "hard-boiled and likable manager," he efficiently ran the Zoo's business, marketing, and entertainment operations until 1932. Sol Stephan continued as General Manager, managing the animal collection and general operations.

The growing popularity of automobiles reduced the profitability of streetcars. The Cincinnati Traction Company was unable to support the Zoo further and the Zoo was sold to civic-minded philanthropists in 1917.

Mr. and Mrs. Charles Phelps Taft (Anna Sinton Taft) were prominent civic leaders. He was one of the Zoo's founding Board members and President from 1917 to 1929. Anna Sinton Taft and Mary M. Emery purchased the Zoo in 1916. (Courtesy of the Taft Museum- details of portraits by Raimundo de Madrazo)

Mrs. Mary M. Emery was a generous local philanthropist, who supported a number of institutions including the Emery Theater, the Cincinnati Art Museum, and the model community of Mariemont. (Courtesy of the Cincinnati Art Museum- detail of Portrait of Mrs. Mary M. Emery by Dixie Selden)

Secretary bird. These unusual long-legged relatives of falcons and hawks feed on snakes and other small prey, which they stamp on with their feet. A pair of the birds was an attraction for many years, especially when they were fed live snakes. The Zoo was one of the first in the country to exhibit this species.

Indian Rhinoceros. A female was purchased in 1922 from the Maharajah of Nepal, via the Hagenbecks, for $10,000. It was apparently the first Indian rhino imported into the country in fifteen years.

The Animal Collection

The Cincinnati Zoo maintained its position as a leading American zoo in spite of its financial difficulties. In 1916 Dr. R. W. Shufeldt wrote in the *Scientific American Supplement* that the Cincinnati Zoo was probably second in importance only to New York's Bronx Zoo. In the early 1920s the *Cleveland Plain Dealer* called the Cincinnati Zoo one of the finest zoos in the world. In 1920 Heinrich Hagenbeck said the Zoo's animal collection was far superior to any other in the United States because of the outstanding health and condition of its 1600 animals. Superintendent Sol Stephan reported in 1923 that, "At no previous time has the Garden exhibited a more extensive or finer collection."

The rare animal species exhibited included Indian rhinoceros, sable antelope, pygmy hippopotamus, secretary birds, even a manatee. Sol Stephan was especially proud of the Zoo's female Indian rhino, which was acquired from the Maharajah of Nepal via the Hagenbeck firm for $10,000 in 1923. It was the first Indian rhino imported into the country in fifteen years. Stephan said that rhinos were "... the greatest attraction a zoo can have." He tried unsuccessfully to get a mate for her. Stephan liked deer and claimed that the Zoo had "...the finest collection of these beautiful animals to be found anywhere." In 1916 the Zoo also boasted of having the finest lion, the biggest polar bear, the smallest zebu cattle, the longest python and alligator, and the tamest elephant in the U. S. Its herd of bison was claimed as the largest at a U.S. zoo. By the early 1930s most of the bison in European zoos had apparently come from the Cincinnati Zoo. Animal health care was improved in 1922 when an animal hospital facility was added on the north side of the original Monkey House (now the Reptile House).

New animal species were continually added to the collection. As much as $18,000 (equivalent to $350,000 today) was spent annually on new acquisitions. These funds generally came from sales of surplus animals bred at the Zoo. Surplus animals were also traded to other zoos. One newspaper wrote regarding the anticipated sale of two storks: "Two storks, $75 each--total $150. Now if you are really in need of a stork and had gone to Sol Stephan, Superintendent of the Zoo, and contracted for the two expected storks in advance last week, you could have gotten them for $65 apiece. But this week the price is $75, and not a cent less. Maybe they will be $95 each next week." You had to be sharp to deal with Sol Stephan!

Zoo Management, Zoo Politics

Sol Stephan was known for his robust energy even in his late 60s. According to the *Cleveland Plain Dealer*, "If ever you are invited to go round the Cincinnati Zoo with Sol Stephan, wear marching shoes and be in good shape. He shakes a wicked walk." Stephan lived in a house on Erkenbrecher Avenue next to the Elephant House. He arrived at work at 6:30 or 7:00 a.m. and "...usually got home by 9 at night." Not until the later years of his career did he take time off from work to go on vacations. By then Sol Stephan's son, Joseph, assisted him as Assistant General Manager.

Sol Stephan became a patriarchal figure locally and in the zoo world. He was often visited and consulted by officials of other zoos, most of whom were also his good friends. According to the *Cleveland Plain Dealer*, Stephan's advice and criticism was blunt yet always kindly and understanding. Around Cincinnati he was called the "Colonel." The Zoo guidebook glowingly described his contributions: "a man of genius came along...when you see the man, you see the Zoo, his lengthened shadow."

During and after World War I there were bitter anti-German feelings across America. After the war German identity and language began to disappear from local culture in Cincinnati and throughout the country. Several leading American zoos, led by William T. Hornaday, Director of the Bronx Zoo, strongly opposed the German Hagenbecks, their animal sales business, and their barless exhibits. This opposition slowed the development of barless, naturalistic exhibits in a number of American zoos for decades.

Sol Stephan was called the "Colonel" in his later years. He was a familiar sight at the Zoo in his pony cart, pulled by his mule "Cy." (Courtesy of the Cincinnati Post)

Joseph Stephan and giant anteater from South America. As Assistant General Manager he assisted his father in managing the Zoo's operations and animal collection.

The Zoo As a Cultural and Civic Center

In keeping with its early German influences, musical performances were always a part of the Zoo's summer season. After World War I there was a great interest in the performing arts in the United States, and a number of summer musical events began across the United States. Both Mrs. Taft and Mrs. Emery were dedicated patrons of classical music. They brought the Cincinnati Symphony Orchestra to the Zoo for outdoor summer concerts and later added opera performances. Grand opera was so popular that the first full opera season began in 1920 under the direction of Ralph Lyford with forty-two performances in seven weeks. The Zoo Opera, or the Cincinnati Summer Opera as it was properly called, became the only major summer opera in the country and operated independently of the Zoo with a separate Board.

Later operatic performances with leading New York Metropolitan Opera performers were of such outstanding quality that beginning in 1923 they were broadcast regionally on the WLW radio station, owned by Powel Crosley, Jr. In the 1930s Summer Opera performances were broadcast nationally by the National Broadcasting Company. According to a later recollection in the *Cincinnati Post*, "It was strictly black tie then, a glamorous full dress affair and social excursion of considerable importance, not the least part of which was dining in the Clubhouse where a table overlooking the audience and the stage below was more vital to society than one of the better boxes." The Zoo Summer Opera developed into a major

musical organization, world famous for both its musical quality and its interactions with animals. During the Zoo Opera's early years Superintendent Sol Stephan later recalled that he had to keep his huge male lion, "Nero," inside the Carnivora House during performances because Nero's tremendous roaring got on a prima donna's nerves. The peacocks also had to be caught and silenced inside a zoo building. Within a few years, however, both performers and audiences accepted and expected the animals' noisy roars, hoots, barks, and wild calls as amusing parts of the musical performances.

In the 1920s the Cincinnati Zoo proudly claimed that it was the only zoo "in the United States combining high class entertainment features with the animal collection." Other musical events included a forty-five player orchestra from the Cincinnati Symphony as well as ballet and dance. Zoo Secretary and Business Manager Charles Miller built the first outdoor ice rink in the nation and began popular ice skating shows. According to local historian Joseph E. Holliday, "Thus it was possible for patrons to come to the Zoo early in the day to observe the animals, hear a symphony concert in the afternoon, enjoy a full-course dinner at the clubhouse for only $1.75, then hear an opera, and during the opera's intermission see Norwegian or Swedish stars and comedy teams skate in the late ice show." Charles Miller added other attractions including amusement rides, a dance pavilion, and a food show that was a major summer event at the Zoo for 50 years. Miller also served as Business Manager for the Opera.

Zoo Opera Pavilion and Clubhouse. Attending the Opera was an elegant Cincinnati event for many years. In the late 1920s a fashionable open-air Opera Pavilion joined the Clubhouse (on the left) and the band shell stage (on the right). The Neo-Classical design was by architects Elzner & Anderson, who had earlier designed the band shell and the Elephant House.

The Clubhouse was an important local center for many decades, hosting many civic, political, and scientific dinner meetings.

The old Clubhouse or Restaurant was described by a local newspaper as "...the scene of many notable occasions. In its dining hall there have been staged sumptuous banquets, with the near-by lion's roars drowning the voices of distinguished after-dinner speakers. The feet of thousands upon thousands of Cincinnatians have made its sturdy floors squeak and creak during its many decades of graceful service." The *Cleveland Plain Dealer* reported, "Sit here a week and the chances are you will have seen everyone worth seeing in Cincinnati. Big historical political gatherings have met here and feasted and fought. Great scientific organizations have met here and dissected fried chicken and talked big scientific talk."

The Cincinnati Zoo had then played an vital role in the life of Cincinnati for many years, serving as an important educational and recreational institution and as a civic center. The *Cincinnati Times-Star* wrote in 1931, "It is doubtful if any Cincinnati institution is closer to the people than the Zoo. It is an old friend whose value to the city is universally recognized." Furthermore, the Cincinnati Zoo had also served the surrounding region, as well as attracting tourists to Cincinnati. The *Dayton Daily News* stated in 1937, "The Zoo has been for at least a half-century the magnet that has drawn millions of people from all over the midwest to the city it has done much to make famous."

An early Food and Home Show. The Food and Home Show was a popular August event for over fifty years. Dozens of booths displayed their wares, sold tasty foods, and offered promotional samples and prizes.

Attendance: Attention to Dollars and Cents

Annual attendance from 1915 to 1918 remained around 275,000 despite the effects of the earlier recession and the outbreak of World War I. After the war, the Zoo's popularity and attendance soared. By 1920 paid attendance had almost doubled to 518,216. Zoo officials attributed this rise to a national postwar desire for entertainment. Through the "Roaring 20s" attendance continued to rise. In 1926 it reached 746,000. While attendance grew swiftly, the admission price remained what it had been since opening day fifty years earlier: 25 cents for adults and 10 cents for children.

Success at the gate was unable to meet the high operational expenses, particularly for the costly entertainment events. Little money remained for maintenance and capital improvements. Consequently, there were practically no new animal exhibits or buildings constructed in the 1920s, and none of the barless Hagenbeck-style exhibits which were beginning to appear at several new American zoos. The Zoo's fifty-year-old buildings were now showing their age. After the stock market crash of 1929 and the resulting Great Depression, the Cincinnati Zoo was again financially threatened.

Asking the stork for a baby brother

Zoo guidebook illustration.

Ice cream, peanuts, soft drinks, and picnics have always been an important part of the zoo experience for kids of all ages. (Courtesy of The Cincinnati Historical Society)

Baby pygmy hippopotamus. Pygmy hippos were quite rare in zoos in the 1920s. Zoo babies have always provided newspapers with popular human interest stories and photographs.

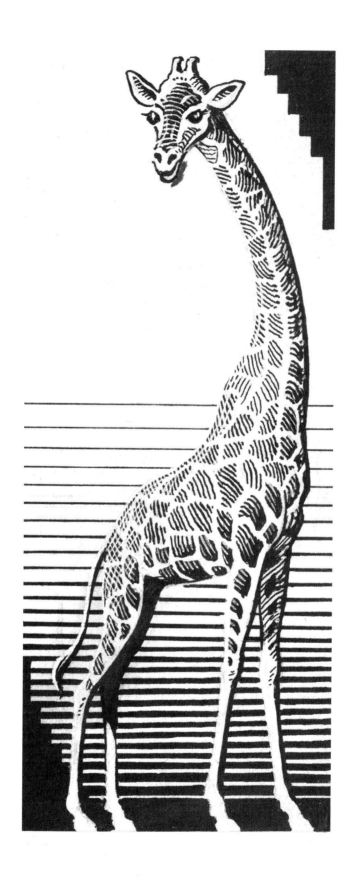

Graphic illustration.

Progress and Growth: 1932-1939

The future of the Cincinnati Zoological Garden looked grim in the early years of the Great Depression. During the 1920s Mrs. Anna Sinton Taft and Mrs. Mary M. Emery had covered deficits. After Mrs. Emery died in 1927, her estate helped pay debts for two more years. Mrs. Taft said in 1931 that, if the city of Cincinnati would purchase the Zoo, she would pay any deficits for the year. Once again, a civic campaign began to save the Zoo. On November 3, 1932, the city purchased the Zoo for $325,000 through park bonds and transferred the Zoo property to the Cincinnati Park Board.

A new Zoological Society of Cincinnati was organized as a nonprofit corporation to own and maintain the animal collection and to meet operating expenses without municipal financial support. The incorporation papers were filed on March 11, 1932 by Robert A. Taft, Mrs. Taft's nephew and President William Howard Taft's oldest son. Taft later became a prominent U.S. Senator. A contract between the Zoological Society and the city's Board of Park Commissioners to operate the Zoo was signed November 26, 1932. The new Board of Trustees consisted of twenty-six members, five of whom were appointed by the city. The new Board appointed a chief executive officer, Managing Director John A. Seubert. He was replaced in 1935 by the Zoo's accountant, John F. Heusser. Sol Stephan, then 83 years old, was General Superintendent, while his son, Joseph, was Assistant General Superintendent.

Mrs. Lilly Ackerland Fleischmann (on the right) at the Bear Grottos with her son, Julius Fleischmann, Jr. (on the left). Her donations in the 1930s were responsible, along with federal funds, for many new exhibits. In 1937 Mrs. Fleischmann became the Zoo's first female board member.

A New Plan of Zoo Development

The Zoo's original exhibits and buildings were then almost 60 years old and deteriorating. Major new exhibits had not been built in years. The animal collection was aging. Although the Cincinnati Zoo had always been a leading zoo, it was being passed up by new zoos in St. Louis, Detroit, and Chicago, as well as the revitalized National Zoo in Washington, D.C.

The new Zoo Board under President James A. Reilly and Park Board President Irwin M. Krohn adopted an aggressive program of capital improvements. The scope of this comprehensive plan included new state-of-the-art exhibits, visitor facilities, parking, paving, new water mains, building repair, and hundreds of new trees and shrubs. Although funding for new exhibits came from several donors, the principal benefactor was Mrs. Lilly Ackerland Fleischmann. Donations were matched by Federal W.P.A. and P.W.A. employment funding. Like a number of American zoos, the Cincinnati Zoo greatly benefited from depression-era federal employment programs. Later in 1937, Mrs. Fleischmann became the Zoo's first female board member. Prominent citizens Irene Gibson Emery (Mrs. John J.) and Jean Maxwell Schmidlapp (Mrs. Horace) organized efforts to preserve the Zoo Summer Opera during the difficult years of the Depression.

Advocates of Barless Exhibits. Left to right, Walter A. Draper, long-time Board member; Sol A. Stephan, Zoo General Manager; Lorenz Hagenbeck, the youngest son of Carl Hagenbeck; and Dr. Sol G. Stephan, Sol Stephan's grandson and Zoo Veterinarian.

The Zoo Goes Wild: Barless, Naturalistic Exhibits

Sol Stephan and his son Joe had long dreamed of building barless, Hagenbeck-style animal exhibits using artificial rockwork construction. A step was taken in 1930 when the moated "Monkey Island" was built next to the Monkey House (now the Reptile House), but the design was not very naturalistic. In 1933 the new Board of Trustees adopted a policy of eliminating bars and cages as much as possible in its renovation program. The Hagenbeck firm was brought in to design a series of new barless, naturalistic exhibits. The Hagenbeck sculptor, Joseph Pallenberg, completed the Lion and Tiger Grottos and an adjacent bird exhibit in 1934 at a cost of $2,500. Pallenberg later worked on the construction of the new Detroit Zoo, which was directed by the Stephans' good friend and former Hagenbeck employee John Millen. Cincinnati's new big cat exhibits were connected to the Carnivora House by a 100-foot tunnel designed by the local architectural firm Fechheimer & Ihorst along with the Stephans. The construction of the Hagenbeck-designed African Veldt (1934) and Bear Grottos (1937) was directed by Carl Kern, a local Swiss-trained landscaper, who also created the rocky landscape of Cincinnati's Krohn Conservatory. The Zoo's hilly site was utilized to its best advantage by the Hagenbeck firm. The bear and cat exhibits were placed in steep hillsides, blending the artificial rockwork with the surrounding landscape.

The Tiger Grotto opened in 1934. The five new tigers in the new barless exhibits were purchased from the Hagenbeck firm. They were donations of Board member and grocer B. H. Kroger. A number of other animals for the Zoo's new exhibits were donated by prominent Board members.

Artificial rockwork construction involves spraying wet concrete or "gunite" onto a fabricated metal framework. The wet concrete is artistically sculpted into rock forms. Later the artificial rock is carefully stained to simulate natural landforms. In this photo Sol G. Stephan (on the left), grandson of Sol Stephan, brushes wet gunite. Stephan, then a veterinary student, worked under the direction of Hagenbeck designer and sculptor Joseph Pallenberg. The first large-scale zoo usage of this technology was at Hagenbeck's Tierpark.

Kodiak bears at the Bear Grottos. This exhibit opened in 1937 at a cost of $104,000. Kodiak bears are among the largest bears in the world. "Admiral," the large male, on the left, weighed over 1, 500 lbs. It was apparently the largest bear in captivity. It was named in 1934 by Dr. W. Reid Blair, Director of the New York Zoological Park. (Courtesy of Pamela L. Brown)

ANTELOPE, ZOOLOGICAL GARDENS, CINCINNATI, OHIO   E-446

Out of Africa

The African Veldt was a particularly innovative exhibit that was built in 1935. It replaced a hoofed animal exhibit that had opened in 1875 as the Deer House. The Veldt was designed by Joseph Pallenberg of the Hagenbeck firm, assisted by Joe Stephan. Antelope, zebra, and birds were displayed together on a spacious three-and-a-half acre plateau. The Veldt featured two "water holes" and a dramatic African rock outcrop or "kopje" constructed of artificial rockwork that covered a shelter barn. Rocky outcrops along the Kentucky River near Lexington, Kentucky, were studied by Joseph Pallenberg, Joe Stephan, and Carl Kern, the construction manager, to add realism. Over 300 federally-funded Civil Work Administration workers labored five months, removing vast quantities of soil for the project. Lorenz Hagenbeck said that there was nothing like Cincinnati's African Veldt in the zoo world. The Director of the Berlin Zoo, Dr. Lutz Heck, studied the exhibit in a 1935 visit. He said that it was the most dramatic and educational exhibit in the world and added that he wished to construct a similar display in Berlin. With the completion of these barless exhibits Cincinnati joined the Detroit Zoo, Chicago's Brookfield Zoo, and the St. Louis Zoo as leaders in the trend toward naturalism in zoos.

The African Veldt opened in 1935, featuring antelope, zebra, and a variety of birds in a spacious setting.

Landscape: Old and New

In 1934 the *Cincinnati Enquirer* described the Zoo as "known far and wide for three predominate features - its fine collection of animals, its equally interesting groups of native and foreign trees, and its summer season of grand opera." The Zoo's botanical beauty was enhanced by the Cincinnati Park Board, under its President Irwin Krohn and Horticulturist Harry Gray. Hundreds of trees, shrubs, and wildflowers were planted at the new exhibits and throughout the Zoo grounds. Landscaper Carl Kern was also involved in many plantings. Visiting zoo officials, such as the National Zoo's Dr. William Mann, the Bronx Zoo's Dr. W. Reid Blair, and the St. Louis Zoo's William Dieckman, applauded varied aspects of the Zoo's landscape from its mature trees to its hilly site. Dieckman said that he thought that the grounds were the most beautiful of any zoo that he knew. German-born Head Gardener Henry Wiesenmaier carefully supervised the Zoo's gardens from 1937 until 1962.

New landscaping. Hundreds of trees and shrubs were planted by the Cincinnati Park Board at new exhibits and gardens and throughout the grounds. The Zoo was regionally known for its outstanding collection of trees and shrubs.

A New Exhibit at Cincinnati

Except for alligators, some local snakes, a few cobras, and giant pythons, reptiles were a group of animals that the Zoo had never been able to exhibit. Sol Stephan had wanted to build a large reptile house as early as 1893 but funding was not available. In the 1920s several other major American zoos built new exhibit buildings devoted to reptiles. They proved to be very popular and helped to change public attitudes about these often-maligned animals. In contrast to the spacious outdoor Hagenbeck exhibits, this type of display was small and indoors. It was based on natural history museum dioramas using painted mural backgrounds, live plants, logs, and rocks along with the animals.

In 1937 Cincinnati's first "Reptile House" opened at a cost of $135,000, financed through private and federal funding. It was patterned after similar buildings in St. Louis, Philadelphia, Toledo, New York, and Washington, D.C. The local architectural firm of Fechheimer & Ihorst designed the building in the characteristic Moderne or Depression Modern style of 1930s New Deal public architecture. It featured a symmetrical form with streamlined details, including Art Deco-style aluminum grillwork. This sparse, geometric style evoked the era's progressive and technological hopes. In contrast to the naturalistic design of the barless Hagenbeck exhibits, however, the austere Moderne style was not suited to expressing the essential natural character of zoos.

Dr. Sol G. Stephan was the grandson of General Manager Sol A. Stephan and served as Zoo Veterinarian and Curator of Reptiles. Here, Stephan treats a cobra for a skin problem, assisted by keeper Millard Owens.

Among the building's first inhabitants were a variety of reptiles, including rattlesnakes that Joe Stephan, Assistant General Manager, had collected in Arizona and Northern Mexico. His son, Sol Stephan's grandson, Dr. Sol G. Stephan, was hired as the Zoo's Veterinarian and also acted as Curator of Reptiles. In 1953 the Reptile House was converted into today's Bird House and the original Monkey House became the Reptile House of today.

The Reptile House. Reptile exhibit buildings were popular at zoos in the 1920s and 1930s and helped to change public attitudes about reptiles. Cincinnati's building opened in 1937 at a cost of $135,000. In 1953 the building was converted into the Bird House of today.

Popular Attractions

"Susie," a trained female gorilla, was a star attraction for sixteen years. She was captured as an infant in the Belgian Congo, displayed in Europe, and flown over the Atlantic Ocean on the Graf Zeppelin. She was later purchased by Board member Robert J. Sullivan and placed at the Zoo in 1931. She and her trainer, William Dressman, had meals together seated at a table with cups, plates, and spoons. Susie's birthday was celebrated on August 7 and children attending her birthday party received cake and ice cream, while Susie was the recipient of a variety of gifts, including fruit baskets, nuts, and candy. Dressman's wife, Carolyn, trained chimpanzees to roller skate and ride tricycles at daily shows.

"Pygmy" African forest elephant and keeper. "Gimpy" was a popular animal at the Zoo for many years. At maturity she was only six feet tall and weighed 2,500 pounds. Pygmy elephants were then considered a small subspecies of the forest elephant. Today however, they are considered to be only small individual animals. Gimpy was donated in 1932 by Judge Alfred K. Nippert. The keeper in this photo is Ed Coyne, who started working at the Zoo in 1877 at the age of ten.

Elephant seal, 1933. "Goliath" was loaned to the Zoo by the Ringling Circus in the summer of 1933. Elephant seals are the largest of the seals and sea lions. Males grow up to 17 feet long and can weigh 2 1/2 tons.

A Renewed Zoo

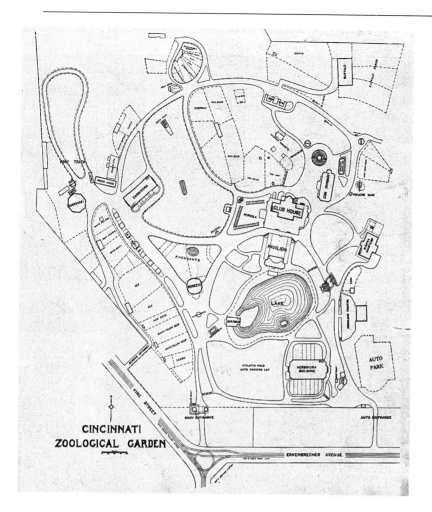

Map of the Zoo in 1942. By the end of the 1930s much of the Zoo had been renewed. The Zoo resumed its place among the nation's leading zoos.

By the end of the 1930s much of the Zoo had been renewed through a combination of private and government funding. The old Clubhouse, which had hosted fashionable events for decades, was razed in 1937. In its place more opera seating was added and the first Children's Zoo was constructed. One of the world's early children's zoos, it has been rebuilt several times since. A new "Dairy Bar" restaurant was constructed in 1938. It is the Zoo Restaurant of today. New parking lots, paving, water mains, concession stands, and an animal hospital were other legacies of this ambitious era when the Cincinnati Zoo resumed its place among the nation's leading zoos.

Visitor attendance declined in the early 1930s from a high of 744,000 in 1930. Later it rebounded to 663,000 in 1937, although bad weather caused a decline the next two years to 593,000. Admission remained at 25 cents for adults and 10 cents for children as it had been since the 1870s. The Zoo was a major tourist destination for the region and promoted attendance with a variety of shows, events, group programs, and Kiddieland amusement rides. Longtime Public Relations Manager Ned Hastings generated a constant flurry of newspaper coverage with a mixture of announcements and human interest animal stories.

The Zoo considered itself an educational institution for adults as well as children. It was proud to be known as "An Open Air University." Animal exhibits were labeled, as were many of the trees throughout the grounds. In 1934 an educationally-oriented radio program, "Uncle Steph's Zoo Club," was organized for children between the ages of four and fourteen. During the summers Boy Scouts gave weekend tours to visitors. The boys were selected from troops throughout Hamilton County and completed a special training course during the winter. In the late 1930s a series of school tours were organized over a six-week period in May-June for ninety thousand school children with their teachers and parents.

Come Up Sometime And See Me In My Bar-less Cage

I'm home most all the time. Enjoy a wholesome day in a healthful atmosphere.

At the ZOO

Sol Stephan Retires

On September 18, 1937, Sol Stephan retired at age 88 on the Zoo's 62nd anniversary. His professional career working with animals began as a youth during the Civil War and ended 75 years later on the eve of World War II. Sol Stephan had become a legendary figure in the zoo world, renowned for his expertise in animal management and breeding. He was named General Manager Emeritus, with his son, Joseph Stephan, replacing him as General Manager. Earlier, at the dedication of Chicago's Brookfield Zoo in 1934, its Director, Edward Bean, specially honored Stephan for his longevity as a zoo director. In 1936 John Millen, Director of the Detroit Zoo, wrote to Lorenz and Heinrich Hagenbeck, "I have always considered your father (Carl) the father of all animal men, and next to him my greatest admiration is for Sol Stephan." Zoos in San Diego, Cleveland, Columbus, and St. Louis sought advice and information from the "Colonel" well past his 80th birthday. Locally, Sol Stephan was a well-loved celebrity. Dr. Roger Conant, former Director of the Philadelphia Zoo, recalled, "Everyone knew him, had heard about him, or had seen his picture in the newspaper." In 1930 the *Cincinnati Times-Star* ran a colorful series of fifty articles by noted newswriter Frank Y. Grayson about Stephan and the Zoo with many of Stephan's stories and reminiscences. Stephan was later described by another newspaper reporter as having "... grown into a Churchillian figure whose know-how, witticisms, kindliness and fund of animal tales endeared him to everyone." On his retirement a memorial plaque was dedicated. It featured a relief by noted sculptor Louise Abel. Mounted on a massive granite boulder, it now is located by today's Reptile House.

One of America's pioneer zoo directors, Sol Stephan had early insights regarding zoos and animal management that seem remarkable today. He advocated that zoos exchange animals for breeding to increase genetic diversity. Stephan viewed zoos as repositories of endangered species and of those species extinct in the wild. He predicted that zoos of the future would be barless and cageless in design. Stephan was acknowledged by many others in the zoo profession for influencing their careers. On retiring, he expressed satisfaction that zoos were becoming regarded as educational institutions rather than as menageries for entertainment. Sol Stephan played an important role in the development both of American zoos and of the role of the modern zoo director. Much of the Cincinnati Zoo's early success was a reflection of Stephan's effort, wisdom, and determination.

Sol Stephan with a baby African elephant. Stephan retired at the age of 88 in 1937. He had worked at the Zoo for 62 years since its opening in 1875 and directed it for 51 of those years. He was a pioneer in the zoo world, renowned for his knowledge of animals and zoo management.

Asian Elephant and trainer. *Photograph taken by well-known local photographer Paul Briol.*

Modernizing the Zoo: The 1940s & 1950s

The last of the federally-funded depression-era projects was opened in 1942 with the renovation of the hoofed animal exhibits near the Zoo entrance on Vine Street. During World War II, many Zoo operations were disrupted by reductions in supplies, materials, and labor. Wartime gasoline and tire rationing caused a drop in attendance, especially from outlying areas and schools. Visits declined from 656,000 in 1941 to 376,000 in 1943, rebounding to almost 500,000 in 1945. By 1943 the size of the animal collection had also decreased to fewer than 1,100 specimens. During a fire at the African Veldt in 1942 ten antelope and two zebras were lost. Among the staff who entered the military was Zoo Veterinarian Dr. Sol G. Stephan. Earlier, in 1940, he was elected Chairman of the American Association of Zoological Parks and Aquariums, but was unable to continue because of military service. During the war his father, General Manager Joseph Stephan, was in charge not only of the animal collection but also of a vegetable garden for the animals called "Crops for Critters." In 1943 the Food and Home Show, first held in 1918, was suspended for a "Win the War Exhibition" in which the armed services displayed aircraft, artillery, and other military equipment.

During the 1940s entertainment became more popular at the Zoo, especially animal shows. Chimpanzees roller skated and rode tricycles, while "Susie," the gorilla, seated with her trainer, continued her daily meals to the delight of thousands. Susie was a crowd pleaser who interacted with the throngs gathered around her.

Hoofed animal exhibits, later called the "Deer Line," were opened in 1942 near the Vine Street entrance at a cost of $100,000. They were the last exhibits built at the Zoo before the outbreak of World War II.

The Heyday of the Zoo Opera

The wartime was the heyday of the Zoo Summer Opera. With many European stars unable to perform in Europe and stranded in the United States, operatic quality at the Zoo reached its peak. Attendance was likewise high during the eight-week summer season. Some of the era's noteworthy debuts included performances by Rise Stevens, Grace Moore, and Jeanette McDonald, along with such notable performances as *Tosca* in 1948 with Richard Tucker and Stella Roman. Opera singers continued to compete with choruses by the Zoo's lions, peacocks, donkeys, and ducks to the delight of audiences. According to a later article in *Theater Arts* magazine, "In Cincinnati a visiting opera star may find herself doing a duet with a lion or singing with a chorus of monkeys...." In addition, opera singers also had to contend with low-flying moths, mosquitoes, and other insects. Both the animal life and the equally unpredictable Cincinnati weather gave opera-goers memorable experiences for many years. For patrons unwilling to pay for seats in the Pavilion there were dozens of free park benches outside where the music, a picnic dinner, and a summer evening at the Zoo could be enjoyed.

The Zoo Summer Opera. The wartime was the heyday of the Zoo Summer Opera. With many European stars stranded in the U.S.A., the Zoo's operatic performances were outstanding. (Courtesy of the Cincinnati Opera)

After the War

The progress in renovating the Zoo that had occurred before the war was again resumed. Plans for renewal were ambitiously made by the Board under President James A. Reilly and Cincinnati Park Board President Irwin M. Krohn, who also served on the Zoo Board as Chairman of Buildings and Grounds. A master plan for future development was produced, working with local architects Kruckemeyer & Strong. The Children's Zoo was renovated in 1947 in time to be used by a new generation of post-war "baby boomers." In 1949 $500,000 in city bonds were allocated for a new Carnivora House, an Ape House with an amphitheater, a renovated sea lion exhibit, and other improvements. In contrast to other municipally supported zoos, however, the Cincinnati Zoo received only a small amount of funding from the city, ranging from $5,000 to $25,000. In 1949 visitor attendance reached 743,916.

In 1947 Susie, the Zoo's female gorilla, died from a bacterial disease, leptospirosis. At the age of twenty-two Susie was one of the oldest gorillas in captivity. She was also one of the Zoo's all-time most popular animals and the news of her death captured the headlines of local newspapers.

The 1940s marked the end of a long era of continuous service by key zoo personnel. One of the most popular keepers, Ed Coyne, died in 1942. He started working at the Zoo as a boy of 10 in 1877 and worked for 65 years until his death at the age of 75. He had been the elephant trainer for many years as well as a keeper at the Elephant House. After the war Dr. Sol G. Stephan returned to the Zoo as its veterinarian, but left after a couple of years to go into private practice. On April 3, 1949, his renowned grandfather, Sol A. Stephan, was 100 years old. He was called "the venerable dean of American zoo administrators" and received congratulatory messages from colleagues and friends throughout the zoo world. Among the many messages was one from Dr. Jean Delacour, famed French ornithologist, then a research associate at the American Museum of Natural History: "Your work at Cincinnati has been remarkable, and you can be proud of it. The excellent Zoological Garden that you have created has the unique feature of being altogether representative of the modern techniques of the New World as well as of the charm and style of the Old World." Dr. William Mann, the Director of the National Zoo in Washington, D.C., wrote to Sol Stephan, "As you are the oldest and most experienced zoological park director, and as you are the first "zoo man" that I ever knew as a boy, I wish to congratulate you." In June 1949, Sol Stephan's son, General Manager Joseph Stephan, retired from the Cincinnati Zoo at the age of 69. Later in the year, on October 28, the celebrated Sol Stephan died.

Sea Lion Pool. Several new projects were planned in the late 1940s, including this renovation of the sea lion exhibit.

Bengal tigers in a barless exhibit.

New Directions In Zoo Design

The 1950s began with great promise. The planning of the Zoo Board of Trustees and staff in the late 1940s resulted in the construction of a wide range of new exhibit buildings, service facilities, and other renovations.

The Lilly Ackerland Fleischmann Memorial Aquarium was opened in 1950 in honor of one of the Zoo's great benefactors. It was one of the larger aquariums in the country. The new building exhibited fresh-water fish and other forms of aquatic life that had never before been displayed at the Zoo. Architect Carl A. Strauss and Associates created its unobtrusive, low-slung design to blend harmoniously with the landscape. They also designed the similar Administration Building which extends over Swan Lake. The dedication of this attractive facility in 1953 featured a keynote address by Marlin Perkins, then Director of Chicago's Lincoln Park Zoo and host of the popular T.V. program "Zoo Parade."

Zoo Director John F. ("Jack") Heusser was involved in an ambitious construction program in the early 1950s. Heusser started at the Zoo as a gate attendant and later became the Zoo's accountant. He served as Executive Director for 26 years from 1935 to 1961.

The Fleischmann Aquarium opened in 1950 in memory of Mrs. Lilly Ackerland Fleischmann, the Zoo's principal benefactor in the 1930s, who died in 1947.

New Hygienic Exhibits

Advances in veterinary medicine led to a greater awareness of diseases and the importance of sanitation in zoos. The result was a new kind of zoo design which emphasized easily cleanable, sanitary exhibits. The old Carnivora House, built in 1875, was replaced in 1952 by a new brick building at a cost of $250,000. The new Carnivora House or "Lion House" and the similar Ape House, which was finished in 1951, were designed by architects Kruckemeyer & Strong. The new buildings had indoor cages with tile walls and stainless steel caging, which could be readily cleaned and sterilized. The design of these new exhibits was not naturalistic and was a radical departure from the earlier indoor diorama-style exhibits at the Reptile House completed in 1936.

An amphitheater and stage were built on the south side of the Ape House for trained animal shows, which had become very popular in many American zoos. The amphitheater opened August 7, 1950 at the Zoo's week-long Diamond Jubilee, celebrating its 75th anniversary. On its last day the Jubilee attracted 26,192 paid admissions, one of the highest attendance figures in the Zoo's history.

In 1952 young Cecil Jackson was hired at the Zoo and soon became involved in training animals. Through the years he has become a familiar fixture at the Cincinnati Zoo with his animal shows, elephant rides, and many public appearances.

Lioness and cubs at the new Carnivora House or "Lion House." The building was completed in 1952 at a cost of $250,000.

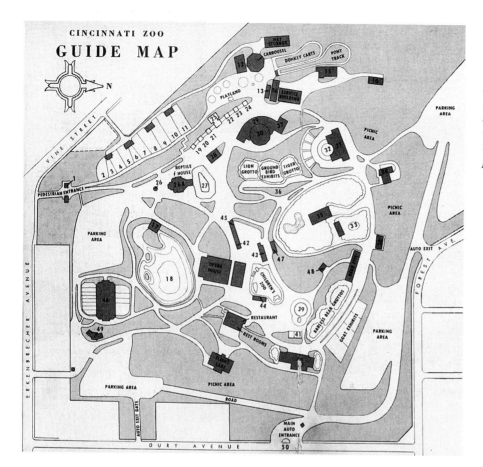

CINCINNATI ZOO
GUIDE MAP

Zoo map, 1958. Many new buildings were built in the early 1950s, including the Aquarium, Ape House, and new Carnivora House. This construction completed twenty years of renovation since the city of Cincinnati purchased the Zoo in 1932.

More Changes and Improvements

In 1951 the sea lion exhibit was again rebuilt on the same site where the first sea lion exhibit was constructed in 1878. The Buffalo Range, which opened at the turn of the century, was converted into a parking lot, and the main automobile entrance was constructed on Dury Ave. The Reptile House, built in 1937, was converted into the Bird House of today in 1951 by Director Jack Heusser, who was especially interested in birds. The Monkey House, erected in 1875, then became the present Reptile House. The monkeys were moved to the seven original Bird Aviary buildings in 1953. A miniature railroad was built in the late 1940s. A tractor train was added in 1951. The miniature railroad was relocated and expanded in 1959. A spectacular railroad trestle was constructed 25 feet high over one end of the African Veldt, and trestles were also built to extend the train ride out over Swan Lake. The Zoo's amusement ride area, now called "Playland," was further developed with new rides in the 1950s. The Zoo Summer Opera continued its summer performances under the long-time musical direction of Fausto

Cleva, who directed from 1934 to 1965. *Aïda* was always a favorite with audiences because an elephant was included in its Triumphal March. Outstanding performers of the era included such stars as Roberta Peters, John Alexander, Robert Merrill and Italo Tajo.

Zoo visitor attendance rose in the early 1950s from 744,000 to almost 939,000 in 1953. During the next four years attendance steadily dropped, apparently due to inclement weather. In an effort to cut costs the Zoo was closed during the winter months from the mid-1950s until the early 1960s. Each May and June thousands of children from area schools visited during "Zoo Days." "The Food and Home Show" became even more popular in the 1950s with the support of Board Treasurer Eugene Zachman, Director Jack Heusser, long-time Public Relations Manager Ned Hastings, and Zoo concessionaire Charles Beal. It attracted up to 150,000 people in the last two weeks of the summer. Up to 160 commercial booths and displays offered a variety of foods, wares, prizes, demonstrations, and entertainment.

The Zoo Opera continued its popular summer performances along the shores of Swan Lake.

The Food and Home Show became even more popular in the 1950s. Festive crowds thronged the Zoo to see demonstrations and entertainment, sample foods, and pick up prizes and other give-aways.

The Animal Collection

One of the outstanding new animal acquisitions of this decade was a young female lowland gorilla, sent to Cincinnati in 1957 by Dr. Albert Schweitzer, the famous medical missionary of West Africa and Nobel Peace Prize winner. The gorilla, named "Penelope," was given to Zoo Veterinarian Dr. Byron Bernard in appreciation for a number of milk goats donated through funds raised by Cincinnati school children and taken to Africa by Dr. Bernard. The Zoo reported that it had to pay an expensive tax to French Equatorial Africa for the gorilla. With the new addition the Zoo then owned two pairs of lowland gorillas. Dr. Bernard was accompanied to Africa by a teenager, Cathryn Hosea. She has since been associated with the Zoo in a variety of capacities and is widely known by her married name, Cathryn H. Hilker.

Clarence White served as Superintendent from 1949 until his retirement in 1962. With the Zoo's emphasis on new construction, however, the overall status of the animal collection continued to stagnate, as it had since the beginning of the war. By the end of the 1950s the animal collection and much of the Zoo was in need of rejuvenation.

The critical importance of conservation to zoos was noted by President Everett W. Townsley in the 1955 Annual Report: "We are now faced with the responsibility of doing all possible for the protection of wild life.... Zoos must give more consideration to the code of objectives and fight more vigorously for the cause of wild life protection."

Penelope, a female gorilla, was a gift of Dr. Albert Schweitzer, the famous medical missionary of West Africa. (Courtesy of the Cincinnati Enquirer)

Aquatic Bird House. Aquatic birds were displayed at this 1952 addition to the largest of the Zoo's original Aviary buildings.

Galapagos tortoise and young admirer.

The Walk-Through Flight Cage opened in 1962 and allowed visitors the opportunity to see free-flying birds in a spacious naturalistic outdoor exhibit.

Transition Time: 1960-1967

The early 1960s brought a period of change at the Zoo. John F. ("Jack") Heusser retired in 1961 at the age of 63, after serving 26 years as Executive Director. He was replaced by William Hoff, who came from Chicago's Lincoln Park Zoo. There Hoff had served as General Curator under its Director, Marlin Perkins. One of Hoff's early decisions was to hire Edward Maruska, also from the Lincoln Park Zoo, as Animal Superintendent in 1962. Hoff and Maruska brought to the Cincinnati Zoo new vision and professionalism which they had gained from their mentor, Marlin Perkins.

A master plan was adopted by the Board in 1960 which resulted in several major projects and a variety of smaller improvements and renovations. Much of the Zoo's construction through the 1960s was by Carl A. Strauss and Associates. In 1960 a service building was constructed next to the Zoo's auto entrance. The outdoor Walk-Through Flight Cage next to the Bird House opened in 1962 at a cost of $40,000. Baboon Island (now Ibex Island) was constructed in 1962 near the Ape House at a cost of $77,000. Monkey Island, built in 1930 next to the Reptile House, was also renovated in 1962. The artificial rockwork at both of these barless exhibits was designed in a rectilinear and unnatural modernistic style popular in zoos in the early 1960s. The old Vine Street pedestrian entrance building was demolished and replaced in 1962 by the present structure. In 1963 the sea lion exhibit was renovated and an underwater viewing area added. During the same year the Administration Building suffered extensive damage in a fire and many old records were lost. The depression-era animal hospital was converted into the Nocturnal House, which opened in 1964. It was one of the earliest exhibits in which the normal day-night light cycle is reversed in darkened displays so that animals active at night can be seen by visitors in the daytime. The Children's Zoo was greatly improved in a 1964 renovation in memory of long-time Zoo supporter Powel Crosley, Jr. The Elephant House also received major repairs in 1964. In 1963 the Zoo adopted a long-term development program, which was later modified. A number of new exhibits, other improvements, and the acquisition of additional property were financed with $2.7 million of city revenue bonds.

The extensive "Whiting Grove" picnic area was opened in 1965 and named after Board President Carson R. Whiting. It was designed by the nationally-known Cincinnati landscape architect Henry Fletcher Kenney. Whiting Grove has hosted innumerable outings and events, including a political rally in 1966 attended by Senator Robert F. Kennedy.

Monkey Island. In 1962 this exhibit was renovated in a rectilinear style popular in zoos in the early 1960s.

Director William Hoff and lion cub. "Bill" Hoff served as Director for six-and-a-half years and initiated a variety of ambitious programs.

Great advances in Zoo education programs began in this period. Director William Hoff inaugurated a weekly television show, "Your Zoo." The program was educationally themed and greatly popularized the Zoo and its animals. General Curator Ed Maruska made significant improvements in the Zoo's interpretive signage. Instructional materials and slide sets were prepared for schools and integrated with guided tours at the Zoo. Guest lecturers gave programs to Zoo members. A geodesic dome, located near the Opera Pavilion, was used as a gift shop and later converted into an educational classroom with audio-visual facilities.

Zoo attendance during the 1960s grew slowly to 750,000 in 1965, rising the following year to 829,000. During this period former animal trainer Rudy Underwood served as Maintenance Supervisor until his retirement in 1972. Major volunteer programs were initiated which have since grown tremendously. In the mid-1960s the Women's Committee began extensive membership programs using hundreds of volunteers to recruit new members. They also started other volunteer activities, such as tour guides, a speaker's bureau, and a gift shop. Director Hoff and Board President Carson Whiting started the Zoo's Safari Club in 1964, offering nature-oriented travel to friends of the Zoo. Public Relations Manager Dorothy Visser developed special events like the "Zoo Arts Festival" and fund-raising events such as "ZooAuc," a gala auction party.

Children's Zoo. In 1964 the Children's Zoo was renovated in memory of long-time Zoo supporter Powel Crosley, Jr.

Animal Collection and Management

General Curator Ed Maruska worked energetically to improve the Zoo's animal management practices: diets were changed, handling practices improved, keepers were retrained, and new staff was hired. One of the new college graduates hired in 1963 was young Bob Lotshaw. Lotshaw has served as General Curator for many years. Veterinary medical care greatly improved under Consulting Veterinarian Dr. Jerry Theobald, who was hired in 1961 and initiated preventive medicine and vaccination programs. Director William Hoff began research programs at the Zoo, working with the University of Cincinnati, the Taft Research Center, and the Cincinnati Department of Public Health.

The family of Board member Oliver M. Gale donated funds in 1963 for a nursery in the Ape House. This facility allowed greatly improved care of young animals neglected by their mothers. The fruits of these improvements in animal management were seen in significant breeding achievements. On March 22, 1964, the first crowned guenon monkey birth in captivity occurred. The Zoo had several black rhinoceros births. By the late 1960s the Zoo's cat collection was considered one of the finest in the world. Fifteen cat species were bred, including the world's first captive birth of sand cats, the western hemisphere's first captive birth of caracals, and births of Persian and snow leopards.

General Curator Ed Maruska led collecting trips to the wilds of southern Mexico and Guatemala in 1965 and 1966. Among the many species collected was a colony of vampire bats. They and their progeny have flourished ever since as popular denizens of the Nocturnal House, feeding on blood provided from local slaughter houses.

Sand Cat. By the late 1960s fifteen cat species were bred at the Zoo, including the first birth of sand cats in captivity in 1969.

The Cincinnati Zoo hosted several hundred professionals from North American zoos in early March 1964 at the Mid-Winter Conference of the American Association of Zoological Parks and Aquariums (AAZPA). By the end of the 1960s, zoos throughout the world assumed a much greater involvement in wildlife conservation through captive breeding of wildlife. At that time the Cincinnati Zoo exhibited 17 species listed as rare or threatened by the International Union for Conservation of Nature and Natural Resources (IUCN).

Collecting Trip to Mexico. Left to right, John Kolman and General Curator Ed Maruska hold a rare Morelet's crocodile; artist John Ruthven; a Mexican guide; and keeper Paul Westerbeck, who restrains another crocodile.

The Gibbon Islands under construction in 1973 on the site of the former Zoo Opera Pavilion. The new barless exhibit opened in spring 1974. (Courtesy of the Cincinnati Enquirer)

New Leadership: 1967-1979

In the fall of 1967 Executive Director William Hoff left to become Director of the St. Louis Zoological Park. General Curator Edward Maruska served as Interim Director before being named Executive Director on May 23, 1968. At the age of 34, Maruska was one of the nation's youngest zoo directors. A life-long animal lover, he was born and raised in Chicago. He spent much of his childhood at its outstanding zoos, especially the Brookfield Zoo with its barless Hagenbeck-designed exhibits. Maruska has always possessed a remarkable enthusiasm for the natural world, especially for rare and unusual animals of all kinds. As a young man he worked in several departments at Chicago's Lincoln Park Zoo before taking charge of the Cincinnati Zoo's animal collection.

As a new zoo director Maruska had an ambitious vision of the Cincinnati Zoo as a great zoo. Maruska's concept of zoo excellence has blended an outstanding collection of animals with naturalistic exhibits, an emphasis on education and science, landscape beauty,

well-maintained order, and a persistent desire to improve. His unique combination of energy, determination, and adaptability has worked over the years to implement and unify the efforts, skills, and resources of many employees, Board members, volunteers, donors, and members.

In 1968 the Goetz Animal Health Center was completed, provided by a bequest of Christian and Emma Goetz. That year Barry Wakeman, the newly-hired Zoologist, went to the Antarctic along with staff from several other zoos on a collecting trip sponsored by the National Science Foundation. He brought back a number of birds, including Emperor and Adélie penguins. These were displayed in a new climate-controlled exhibit, which opened at the Bird House in 1969. Outside this building a large new flight cage was also constructed. Wakeman later initiated education programs, including the on-going Junior Zoologists Club and a local wildlife rescue program for orphaned baby animals.

Goetz Animal Health Center *was completed in 1968, providing modern animal health care facilities at the Zoo.*

At this time property adjacent to the Zoo, which had been originally owned by the Zoo and sold in 1886, was reacquired and developed as badly-needed parking space. This increased the Zoo's grounds from 57 to 65 acres, approximately the size of the Zoo when it opened. Through federal funding one of Cincinnati's first large-scale abstract sculptures, the *Helios Guardians*, was incorporated into the parking area. It was created by sculptor Michael Bigger and dedicated to the memory of Michael Grzimek, the conservationist son of Dr. Bernhard Grzimek, famed zoological authority and Director of the Frankfurt Zoo. The younger Grzimek died in a plane crash in Kenya. The Grzimeks had co-authored the internationally-popular book, *Serengeti Shall Not Die*, which alerted a worldwide audience to the threats to African wildlife from mankind. Dr. Grzimek and Mrs. Michael Grzimek attended the dedication ceremony at the Zoo in the fall of 1969.

In 1969 the last Food and Home Show closed at the Zoo, ending a 51-year late-summer tradition in Cincinnati. According to Board President Oliver Gale, it closed because of "increased costs, changing public tastes, and the growing sophistication of the Zoo itself."

This period also saw the last years of the Cincinnati Summer Opera at the Zoo. Started in the 1920s, it was the second oldest continuing opera company in the country after New York's Metropolitan Opera. By the late 1960s, however, the Zoo Opera's facilities were clearly showing their age. Outstanding singers performed at the Zoo throughout the 1960s, including rising stars Placido Domingo, Sherrill Milnes, Norman Treigle, Elizabeth Schwarzkopf, and Beverly Sills, while James de Blasis made his directing debut with the Opera in 1968.

Often some of the Opera's most memorable performers, of course, continued to be zoo animals with their spontaneous and unpredictable choruses. Beverly Sills recalled in an article in the *Cincinnati Post* that the animals were "... all part of the wonderful atmosphere and the informality of it all." After a sea lion accompanied her during one performance, a newspaper headline read, "*La Traviata* starring Beverly Seals." Of all the animals, the peacocks were the most frequent performers. Sherrill Milnes remembered, "They would call at any time, before the high note, after the high note, in the rests." One of the most amusing animal incidents in the history of the Zoo Summer Opera occurred in 1964 during a performance of Menotti's *The Medium*. At the opera's climactic moment, Madame Flora called out, "Who's there?" Guess who called back?

Peacock. (Courtesy of the Cincinnati Enquirer)

Pygmy Hippopotamus. Outdoor moated exhibits with landscape plantings were completed at the Elephant House in 1971. The Zoo adopted an overall naturalistic style of design for its 1970 Master Plan.

At the end of its first century, the Cincinnati Zoological Garden had a hodgepodge collection of buildings of different ages, styles, and quality, along with acres of concrete and asphalt. Animal exhibits and holding quarters were often small, inadequate, and not very natural looking. The Zoo's landscape had the appearance of an old, but very ordinary, park. Director Ed Maruska and the Board of Trustees embarked on an extensive program to transform the Zoo, naturalizing animal exhibits, and replacing the urban, architectural appearance of the Zoo with thickly-planted landscape.

In 1970 the Zoo Board under President Andrew Hopple adopted a ten-year, ten-million-dollar master plan that was developed with architects Glaser and Myers, Inc. Director Ed Maruska and architect Russell C. Myers developed a naturalistic style of architecture and design with animal exhibits simulating nature as much as possible.

Several exciting outdoor displays were planned, existing exhibits and service buildings of poor quality were demolished, and key elements of the historic architecture were preserved. To improve the Zoo's barren urban appearance conventional architecture was de-emphasized, while new landscape plantings were used to screen buildings, soften harsh man-made surfaces, and give an overall natural feeling and scale. To evoke a wild, exotic ambiance, rough-cut, treated-timber construction was used in exhibits, buildings, and as pathway edging. Both the treated-timber architecture and landscape plantings visually linked and integrated the diverse architectural collection of the Zoo. In the design of animal exhibits and public areas Director Maruska emphasized the importance of gardens and landscape. This emphasis recalls the zoological garden vision of the Zoo's founding fathers and the Hagenbeck realism that the Stephans had followed.

91

The Gibbon Islands replaced the Zoo Summer Opera Pavilion in 1974. After over fifty years of opera at the Zoo the loud hooting calls of the apes succeeded the arias of opera singers.

New Exhibits and Landscape

In 1970 the new Eagle Flight Cage was erected to the west of the Reptile House. This massive structure was 72 feet tall, 140 feet long, and 50 feet wide. In 1971 artificial rockwork, plantings, and a pool were added to outdoor displays at the Elephant House. Below the Elephant House the nineteenth-century cages for birds of prey were beyond repair. In 1972 they were replaced with new bird flight cages.

Throughout its history the Cincinnati Zoo has expanded its collections and exhibits of the world's life forms. In 1973 the Zoo constructed large saltwater tanks in an addition to the Fleischmann Memorial Aquarium. These were accompanied by sophisticated educational signage and graphics regarding ocean life and conservation. Improvements to all of the exhibits in the Aquarium were also made.

The Cincinnati Summer Opera performed its last season at the Zoo in 1971 before moving to the newly renovated Music Hall near downtown. Cincinnatian James Levine conducted the final performance, which was *The Barber of Seville* with Roberta Peters. Levine, who as a boy had grown up with the Zoo Opera, became musical director and later artistic director of the New York Metropolitan Opera. The Zoo Opera Pavilion was demolished in 1972 and replaced by the extensively landscaped Gibbon Islands exhibit, which opened in the spring of 1974.

With the new Master Plan's emphasis on landscaping, in 1974 Dave Ehrlinger was hired as Horticulturist to head the Horticulture Department. The Cincinnati Zoo became one of the first American zoos in many decades to emphasize plants and landscaping. There was a return to the exoticism of the early Zoo, this time with plants and landscaping instead of eclectic architecture. The Zoo soon took on a striking appearance with hardy bamboos, ornamental grasses, summertime plantings of bananas and elephant ears, and hundreds of other plant species. Dozens of unusual species were used to simulate the natural habitats of animals in exhibits. These new informal plantings created a different and exciting zoo landscape, expressive of the exotic character of a zoological garden. By the end of the 1970s the Zoo had received two national awards for landscaping and grounds maintenance.

Lemon shark. In 1973 large saltwater exhibits were added to the Aquarium along with many new species of marine life.

The Outdoor Gorilla Exhibit opened in 1978 to display the Zoo's rapidly expanding gorilla population. It was one of the earliest large naturalistic primate exhibits in the zoo world.

A fenced cheetah exhibit was opened in 1974 near the Children's Zoo with a simulated African landscape planting. In 1976 a Hagenbeck bird exhibit built in 1934 between the Lion and Tiger Grottos was converted into another cheetah display. Several cheetah births resulted from the expanded space, and the Cincinnati Zoo became the third U.S. zoo to breed this rare species successfully.

On its centennial anniversary in 1975, the Zoo's Elephant House, Reptile House, and one of the original Aviaries were placed on the National Register of Historic Places. To celebrate its centennial, the Zoo constructed a spacious new outdoor big cat exhibit, located next to the Aquarium. The new display, called "Big Cat Canyon," featured a wooden boardwalk elevated above the heavily planted, fenced exhibit.

In the early 1970s Zoo officials studied some of the nation's outstanding zoos, parks, and gardens for ideas in future planning and, in particular, for an exhibit for the Zoo's growing population of lowland gorillas. Originally designed as a greenhouse conservatory with African plants, the project became an outdoor display and opened in May 1978. It was one of the zoo world's first large naturalistic gorilla exhibits in which both animals and visitors were surrounded by a simulated African jungle composed of exotic-looking but hardy temperate plants.

The construction of the gorilla exhibit required the demolition of the monkey exhibit buildings and the relocation of the old "Playland" amusement ride area to a peripheral site behind the Nocturnal House. The monkey exhibit buildings were some of the Zoo's original buildings, constructed as aviaries for birds in 1875. It was decided to preserve one of the Japanese pagoda-style aviaries as a memorial to the last passenger pigeon and the last Carolina parakeet in captivity, both of which died in these buildings. The building was redesigned as an interpretive display about these two bird species and other extinct and endangered species. Wildlife artist John Ruthven worked on the development of the exhibit. It opened September 1, 1977, sixty-three years after Martha, the last passenger pigeon, died.

The Passenger Pigeon Memorial. One of the original bird aviary buildings, built in 1875, was preserved as a memorial to passenger pigeons. The last passenger pigeon died in one of these buildings in 1914. The remaining building is now listed on the National Register of Historic Places.

In August 1978 the Cincinnati Zoo became the first U.S. zoo to open a major exhibit building devoted to insects. It was named the World of Insects but is more commonly called the "Insectarium." Its innovative displays, interpretive signage, and graphics were designed by Jerry M. Johnson Productions, Inc., along with Zoo staff members. One of the building's features was the nation's first large indoor walk-through butterfly exhibit with pools, a stream, and lush tropical plants and flowers to feed the butterflies. In 1978 the Zoo received the AAZPA Exhibit Award for this unique facility. Rearing unusual insect species with their complex life cycles, short life spans, and unusual diets has presented great challenges over the years to Zoo entomologists. They have made periodic collecting trips to the tropics for new additions to the Insectarium's displays. In 1978 the Zoo received an AAZPA Bean Award for breeding royal Goliath beetles, followed the next year by another award for breeding giant Asian walking sticks. In 1978 the Zoo also completed new outdoor exhibits at the Carnivora House for its outstanding cat collection.

The Insectarium. This was the first major exhibit building devoted to insects at a U.S. zoo. Innovative signs, graphics, videos, and participatory activities were included in its award-winning design.

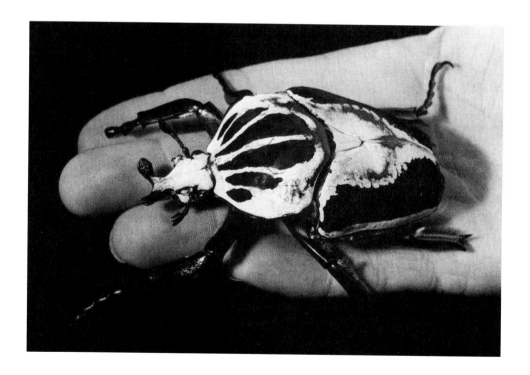

Royal Goliath beetle. The Cincinnati Zoo was the first to breed these five-inch-long African beetles, which feed on ripe fruit as adults.

Baby lowland gorillas with Nursery Keeper Carol Schottelkotte. Since 1970 the Zoo has competed with Chicago's Lincoln Park Zoo for the most gorilla births in zoos.

A New Animal Era

At 7 a.m. on January 23, 1970, Cecil Jackson, Ape House head keeper and animal trainer, witnessed the Zoo's first live lowland gorilla birth: a male, "Sam," born to "Mahari" and "Hatari." This was followed eight days later by a second gorilla birth, a female, "Samantha," born to "Penelope" and "King Tut." The babies were hand-raised by personnel of Good Samaritan Hospital who donated three weeks of their services. Each pair of gorillas continued to produce babies. Both the babies and their parents have been among the most popular of the Zoo's animals. Since the early 1970s the Cincinnati Zoo has competed with Chicago's Lincoln Park Zoo for the most lowland gorilla births in zoos. Another significant birth in 1970 was a Persian leopard, a very rare subspecies of leopard from the Mideast. The baby leopard was delivered by Caesarean section.

Another accomplishment, on June 24, 1970, was the first yellow-headed vulture hatching in captivity. Other especially notable births and hatchings included pampas cats, snow leopards, cheetahs, giraffes, pygmy hippos, bongos, smooth-fronted caimans, and Rothschild's mynahs. In 1974 *Newsweek* magazine called the Cincinnati Zoo "the sexiest zoo in the country" as a tribute to its successful breeding record.

Several young bald eagles have been hatched in different broods since 1979. The young have been released in northern Ohio in cooperation with the Ohio Department of Natural Resources. Reintroducing endangered species into the wild whenever possible is one of the goals of modern zoos.

On June 20, 1974, a Bengal tigress on loan from the National Zoo in Washington, D. C., gave birth to four young: one orange and three white cubs. They were hand reared when their mother refused to care for them. This was the start of a series of white tiger births which has brought much fame to the Zoo. These white tigers are not albinos. They have blue eyes and are generally larger in size than orange-colored Bengal tigers. White Bengal tigers have been seen on rare occasions for centuries in the wilds of northwest India and Bangladesh.

During the Cincinnati Zoo's centennial year in 1975 the white tiger cubs, now practically full grown, were the star attractions of the newly opened Big Cat Canyon exhibit. This litter of tigers eventually went back to the National Zoo, but Director Ed Maruska was able to get permission to breed the mother with a white male tiger on loan from the Cuneo Circus. Another litter of white tigers resulted and the Cincinnati Zoo was able to keep offspring from the litter. White tigers, originating from these animals, have continued to be among the most popular of animals with Zoo visitors ever since.

White Tiger. In 1974 the Cincinnati Zoo had its first litter of white tigers.

The Butterfly Rain Forest exhibit at the Insectarium was the first large indoor walk-through butterfly exhibit at a U.S. zoo. The Insectarium, which opened in 1978, was one of the most innovative of the exhibits constructed during the Zoo renewal that began in the late 1960s.

In 1979 Dr. Lynn Kramer became the Zoo's first full-time veterinarian. He worked closely with Director Ed Maruska, General Curator Bob Lotshaw, and the animal keepers to establish an outstanding animal health program for the rapidly expanding animal collection. Throughout the 1970s the Zoo's animal management practices also continued to improve.

The 1970s initiated a remarkable period of development for American zoos as a whole, with great advances in veterinary medicine, animal management, exhibit design, education, and indeed all aspects of zoo operations. Many new zoos were established and older institutions began ambitious renewal programs. In response to popular opinion, zoos increasingly began to construct larger, barless, naturalistic exhibits and abandoned the small, sterile cages of the previous era. The North American zoo organization, AAZPA, began a rigorous accreditation program to regulate and improve zoo management. The Cincinnati Zoo was accredited in 1976.

Important research in 1978 at the National Zoo in Washington, D.C., clearly demonstrated the dangers of inbreeding in captivity. As a result, a new era of cooperation has developed among the world's zoos in exchanging animals to ensure the genetic health and diversity of their animal populations. In order to manage the transfer of animals for breeding loans and sales, an international data bank of animal genealogy, International Species Inventory System (I.S.I.S.), was created.

A growing awareness of threats to wildlife and the environment resulted in a great increase in federal legislation and regulation with laws such as the Endangered Species Act, and in international agreements like the Convention on International Trade of Endangered Species (CITES). In 1979 the International Union for the Conservation of Nature (IUCN) warned of the threats to natural biodiversity throughout the world. Since then the Cincinnati Zoo has adopted biodiversity as a theme for all of its collections and exhibits.

The Zoo Education Department developed a variety of programs, classes, and tours to foster awareness and concern for wildlife and conservation.

Education at the Zoo

In 1969 the Zoo published a new guidebook, which was written by Zoo Director Ed Maruska. It was intended not only as a guide to the Zoo, but a general introduction to vertebrate animals. Because of the growing role of education in the mission of zoos the Cincinnati Zoo's Education Department was created in 1974. The Zoo's Zoologist, Barry Wakeman, was appointed Curator of Education. A number of innovative programs, classes, and tours soon developed to reach wider audiences of school children and the general public. Well-trained groups of volunteers have been a vital part of educational programs. The Tour Guides have led hundreds of thousands of school children through the Zoo since the 1960s. Beginning in 1970 another group, the "Zoosters," made a variety of handicrafts to sell to benefit Zoo education programs. The "ZOT" (Zoologists Of Tomorrow) summer classes have annually educated hundreds of children through a corps of trained volunteer instructors. In 1975 the Zoo and the Cincinnati Board of Education initiated a vocational high school program, located at the Zoo, that focused on animal care and natural resources. The Zoo's speakers' bureau expanded as did the number of outside programs given by Zoo staff.

Cincinnati's famous international corporate giant, the Procter and Gamble Company, generously donated the Zoo's Education Center, designed by Glaser and Myers, Inc., which opened in 1977 with classrooms, offices, and library. Since 1979 volunteers (later called Zoo Volunteer Interpreters or "Z.V.I.s") have operated summer interpretive stations around the Zoo. University courses relating to the Zoo began at both the University of Cincinnati and Xavier University. A lecture series for members continued with internationally renowned authorities such as gorilla expert Dian Fossey. Since 1977 the Education Department received several AAZPA awards for education programs, including the "Outreach" program sponsored by Frisch's Restaurants. In 1977 the U.S. Department of Health and Welfare in its *American Education* magazine called the Zoo's Education Department the "ultimate model of a Zoo education department."

High school student and calf at the Children's Zoo. A vocational high school program opened at the Zoo in 1975, training students in animal care and natural resource management.

The Zoo Grows

Annual attendance climbed from 798,773 in 1970 to 965,000 in 1979. Zoo attendance was higher than that of all other area cultural institutions, exceeded only by the Cincinnati Reds baseball team and Kings Island theme park. Membership at the Zoo also grew dramatically during this time. Through the energetic efforts of Public Relations Manager James "Pepper" Wilson the Zoo received widespread local and national media coverage. In the late 1970s the Zoo's marketing, advertising, events, and group sales programs expanded greatly under Marketing Director Ted Beattie. The ADOPT program (Animals Depend On People Too) began in 1979 to encourage and involve the public in helping to pay for the rising costs of feeding animals. In 1980 Beattie left the Cincinnati Zoo to become Associate Director of Chicago's Brookfield Zoo. He later was appointed Executive Director of the Knoxville Zoo.

In 1977 the Federal government's Comprehensive Employment and Training Act (CETA) program brought many new personnel to a number of departments, boosting the scope and scale of the Zoo's operations. This was followed in 1979 by another CETA training program. A number of personnel in both programs were later hired by the Zoo.

In 1979 new entrance facilities were constructed adjacent to the Zoo Restaurant with an information center, first aid station, and gift shop. The gift shop or "Zoo Shop" began as a volunteer operation in 1976 and continues to be an important part of the Zoo's operations.

By the late 1970s the Cincinnati Zoo had returned to a position of leadership among the nation's zoos. It had successfully completed a number of major exhibits, created a new Zoo landscape, and achieved outstanding success in its animal breeding and education programs. In 1975 Director Edward J. Maruska was elected to the Board of Directors of the American Association of Zoological Parks and Aquariums. In 1977 he was elected to the prestigious International Union of Directors of Zoological Gardens. In 1978 Maruska was elected to serve as the President of the AAZPA.

Director Ed Maruska and a young Bengal tiger. Since 1968 Maruska has led the Cincinnati Zoo in a wide-ranging program of growth and development.

Red Pandas have been popular animals at the Zoo since 1985.

The Zoo Renewed:
The 1980s and 1990s

After over one hundred years of existence many of the Zoo's buildings, sewers, and its electrical, gas and water supply were in dire need of repair. The Board of Trustees under President William L. Blum decided to seek public funding. In 1982 Hamilton County voters passed a tax levy that brought the Zoo $2 million per year for five years to finance critical rebuilding needs, providing the basis for future growth. In 1986 a renewal tax levy passed. In both elections the levy was approved by over 60% of the voters.

In the 1980s Director Edward Maruska masterminded a comprehensive renovation of most of the Zoo's remaining old exhibits and facilities. During this time practically all the Zoo's buildings and exhibits received major repairs or improvements. Working closely with Maruska and architects Glaser and Myers and

Associates, Inc., Business Manager Jack Huelsman directed private contractors, architects, and the Zoo's exhibit and maintenance departments in designing, constructing, and improving exhibits and facilities throughout the Zoo. In addition, Huelsman also supervised park security, parking, and custodial services. In 1990 Maruska appointed Huelsman as Associate Director. In 1988 Tom Penn retired as Maintenance Supervisor, after serving sixteen years. He was replaced by his assistant, Carl ("Butch") Govreau.

During 1983-1984 major sewer renovation projects and several large-scale construction projects were underway at the same time. Finally, in 1985 four exhibits were completed along with a new Auto Entrance and a renovated Restaurant, resulting in a radically new Zoo.

Renovation. The Carnivora House (or "Lion House"), built in 1952, was transformed into the award-winning "Cat House" in 1985.

The Carnivora House or "Lion House," built in 1950 on the location of the original Carnivora House, was renovated and transformed into the new "Cat House" in 1985. The $1.5 million project was made possible by a number of contributors, spurred on by a $200,000 challenge grant from the Kresge Foundation. The renovation used a theme of "The Cat as a Hunter" and replaced small sterile cages with naturalistic exhibits portraying habitats of cats from around the world. Realistic background murals were painted by John and Emily Agnew. Artificial trees and rockwork were created by the David L. Manwarren Corporation. Museum displays, including saber tooth cat fossils and an ancient mummified Egyptian cat, accompany award-winning graphics and signage. The Cat House renovation earned the Cincinnati Zoo an AAZPA Exhibit Honor award in 1985. Among the species displayed here are the rusty spotted cat, golden cat, pampas cat, Pallas cat, fishing cat, and clouded leopard.

Mother Ocelot and Young. Naturalistic exhibits were created with murals, artificial trees and rocks in the renovation of the Cat House, which opened in 1985.

Penguins. The penguin exhibit is part of the renovated Children's Zoo, which opened in 1985. The Joseph H. Spaulding Children's Zoo includes a nursery, petting pens, and a variety of North American animal exhibits.

The Children's Zoo was completely rebuilt in a $2 million renovation, made possible by Mrs. Ruth Spaulding in memory of her son and husband. The facility, which opened in 1985, includes a nursery, petting pen, small stage and seating area, along with a variety of participatory exhibits, hands-on activities, and a children's gift shop. At the entrance there are outdoor displays of flamingos and black-footed penguins. An area devoted to the western U.S.A. desert has an underground tunnel which children can follow to see animals in their dens and burrows. Another section called the "Eastern Woodlands" features native eastern forest animals in a wooded setting. The educationally oriented Joseph H. Spaulding Children's Zoo operates as a part of the Education Department.

Nearby, the Red Panda Exhibit was completed in 1985 for both subspecies of red pandas, with a naturalistic forest landscape of Chinese plants. The same year Monkey Island was renovated by the Zoo's Exhibit Department staff. This display, located next to the Reptile House, was originally built in 1930.

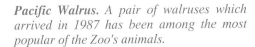

Pacific Walrus. A pair of walruses which arrived in 1987 has been among the most popular of the Zoo's animals.

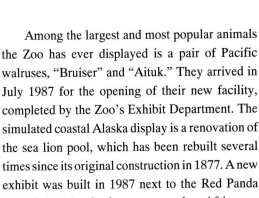

Among the largest and most popular animals the Zoo has ever displayed is a pair of Pacific walruses, "Bruiser" and "Aituk." They arrived in July 1987 for the opening of their new facility, completed by the Zoo's Exhibit Department. The simulated coastal Alaska display is a renovation of the sea lion pool, which has been rebuilt several times since its original construction in 1877. A new exhibit was built in 1987 next to the Red Panda Exhibit for Manchurian cranes, and an African marsh bird display was added as a part of the African Veldt. For the city of Cincinnati's bicentennial year in 1988 a new exhibit, sponsored by Kahn's and Star Bank, was constructed. Here, the Zoo hosted successive visits of a koala from the San Diego Zoo, followed by golden monkeys from China, and, in the fall, a male giant panda belonging to the London Zoological Garden. The panda, "Chia-Chia," was en route from London to a breeding program at the Mexico City's Chapultepec Park Zoo. The profits that the Cincinnati Zoo gained through the record-breaking attendance during the panda's six-week visit went to the Mexican zoo in order to finance the construction of additional panda breeding facilities.

In 1989 the hoofed animal yards called the "Deer Line," near the Vine Street entrance, were overhauled by the Exhibit Department under Allan Sutherland and Earl Wildt. The area had displayed hoofed animals since the Zoo first opened. The renewed exhibit was heavily landscaped and renamed "Wildlife Canyon." It features rare hoofed animal species, including wart hogs, babirusa, anoa, and Sumatran rhinoceros. Along with these major projects a multitude of smaller improvements and construction was completed by keepers, gardeners, maintenance, and exhibit staff.

From the Zoo's original construction in 1875 through the 1960s there were only three major periods of renovation: first, at the turn of the century, the building of the Elephant House and the Buffalo Range; second, in the 1930s the Hagenbeck barless exhibits and the Reptile House and new Restaurant; and, third, in the early 1950s the Aquarium, Ape House, and new Carnivora House. In contrast, Director Ed Maruska's entire administration has been a period of continual renovation and improvement. Beyond mere physical change, since the late 1960s every aspect of the Zoo's functions and operations has dramatically improved.

Throughout its recent renovations, much of the Zoo's historic architecture has been carefully preserved. In 1982 the Elephant House, built in 1906, was renewed through funding from the Procter and Gamble Company. In 1987 the Cincinnati Zoo was designated as a National Historic Landmark by the National Park Service in recognition of its "...national significance in commemorating the history of the U.S.A." This important designation was based on the unique characteristics of the Zoo's oldest historic buildings: the Reptile House and the Passenger Pigeon Memorial, which were constructed for the Zoo's opening in 1875, as well as the Elephant House, which opened in 1906.

Rare and Endangered: The Animal Collection Grows In Diversity

By 1990 the Cincinnati Zoo's animal collection was among the best in the zoo world in diversity and rarity, recalling the outstanding quality of the Zoo in its early decades. Rare species included Pacific walruses, bonobo or pygmy chimpanzees, okapi, shoebill storks, zebra duiker antelopes, douc langur monkeys, Japanese giant salamanders, and Sumatran rhinoceros. Director Ed Maruska accomplished this improvement through trading and selling young born at the Zoo, especially white tigers and lowland gorillas, to other zoos throughout the world. In 1980 the animal collection consisted of 2,000 specimens of 550 vertebrate species, along with almost 10,000 specimens of 123 species of invertebrates, plus 15 colonies of social insects. By 1992 the animal collection grew to over 750 species, including one hundred endangered species.

The Species Survival Program (SSP) of the AAZPA was established in the early 1980s for the inter-zoo management of selected endangered animal species in North American zoos. These species of birds, mammals, and reptiles have a doubtful future in the wild so that captive breeding in zoos may be their only chance of survival. European zoos have established a similar cooperative breeding program. These networks of international cooperative programs have significantly changed the operations and functions of modern zoos. Zoos now closely cooperate in exchanging animals to maintain the long-term genetic and demographic viability of captive populations as wild populations continue to decline.

Rare Species Exhibited since 1987

Sumatran rhinoceros
Okapi
Lord Derby eland
Mhorr's gazelle
Zebra duiker
Pacific walrus
Clouded leopard
Rusty spotted cat
Bonobo chimpanzee
Douc langur
Shoebill stork
Waldrapp ibis
Komodo monitor lizard
Japanese giant salamander

Okapi. These rare animals are the closest living relatives of giraffes. A female okapi was acquired from Zaire in 1987. It was the first okapi captured from the wild in many years and a valuable new bloodline for okapi populations in zoos.

The Cincinnati Zoo and its staff have been involved in a number of SSP breeding programs including snow leopards, lowland gorillas, and red pandas. Director Maruska has been species coordinator of the Black Rhinoceros Committee as well as co-chairman of the Amphibian Committee, and the Bengal and Indo-Chinese Tiger Committee. Director of Research, Dr. Betsy Dresser, is the North American Studbook Keeper of the Black Rhinoceros SSP and Chairperson of the Genome Preservation Group of the IUCN Captive Breeding Specialist Group.

For much of his administration Ed Maruska has maintained one of the largest research collections of salamanders in the zoo world. Maruska's efforts were rewarded in 1980 when the Zoo received an AAZPA Bean award for breeding endangered Texas blind salamanders, which were acquired through the U.S. Department of the Interior and the Texas Department of Wildlife. The Zoo also received the AAZPA Bean award for breeding several other species, including the smooth-fronted caiman (1982), Hercules beetle (1984), and Harlequin beetle (1987). The Zoo has continued its outstanding breeding record with such other species as the rusty spotted cat, clouded leopard, aardvark, spectacled bear, Lord Derby or giant eland, red panda, white-breasted kingfisher, Barrow's goldeneye, crimson rosella, banded linsang, and red ruffed lemur.

Texas blind salamander. The Cincinnati Zoo was the first to breed this small endangered species, which is found only in the vicinity of a few caves near San Marcos, Texas.

The Lord Derby or giant eland is the largest of the antelopes. The bulls of this rare African species may weigh up to 2,000 pounds.

Between the early 1970s and 1993, black rhinoceros populations in Africa dramatically dropped from an estimated 65,000 to only 2,000 because of poaching for the animals' horns. Because of both the drastic plight of the black rhino in the wild and the Cincinnati Zoo's past success in breeding this species, the Zoo has become committed to the captive management of black rhinos and other rhino species.

The Cincinnati Zoo became involved in the Sumatran Rhino Trust, a cooperative program with New York's Bronx Zoo, the San Diego Zoo, the Los Angeles Zoo, and the Indonesian government to rescue the extremely rare Sumatran rhinoceros. Smaller than black rhinos, only 700-900 Sumatran rhinos survive in the dense tropical rain forests of Sumatra. Several of these animals were rescued from a forest which was being lumbered. The Cincinnati Zoo received a female in 1989 and a male two years later. The female rhino, however, died in May 1992. A year later another female rhino was received on loan from the International Wildlife Conservation Park, the new name in 1993 for the New York Zoological Park.

Black rhino and baby. Since the 1960s fifteen black rhino babies have been born at the Cincinnati Zoo, more than any other zoo in the world. Since 1970 black rhino populations have plummeted in the wild because of poaching.

Sumatran Rhinoceros. The Zoo acquired this extremely endangered species of rhino in a cooperative program with the Indonesian government and several other zoos.

By the early 1980s the Zoo needed larger facilities than its 67-acre site to fulfill its commitment to breed endangered species. In 1982 the Zoo was given the 100-acre Anna L. Mast Farm in nearby Clermont County to develop a satellite breeding farm. By 1988 facilities were constructed for the off-exhibit breeding of a number of species. The Zoo has also been involved with other zoos in the development of "The Wilds," a 10,000-acre conservation breeding center in southeastern Ohio.

In April 1980 the Cincinnati Zoo hosted two hundred zoo professionals at the Great Lakes Regional meeting of the AAZPA. Later the Cincinnati Zoo continued its leadership role, hosting several international wildlife conservation conferences. In 1983 the "Reproductive Strategies for Endangered Wildlife" conference was held at the Zoo. This was followed in 1986 by "The African Rhinoceros Workshop." In 1988 the Zoo, along with Kings Island's Wild Animal Habitat, hosted the 5th World Conference on Breeding Endangered Species in Captivity. In 1983 the Cincinnati Zoo became one of the few zoos to become accredited by the American Association of Museums.

In the late 1980s the Zoo added a new position of Area Supervisors to animal management. Area Supervisors served under General Curator Bob Lotshaw, and supervised the departmental head keepers and keepers. Area Supervisors included: Mike Dulaney-primates, small mammals, felines; John Arnett- reptiles, fish; Steve Romo-large mammals; Dave Oehler-birds; and Dave Jardine-bears, sea lions, walruses, and Commissary.

In March 1990 a terrible tragedy occurred at the Cincinnati Zoo when a male polar bear attacked a keeper. The keeper, Laurie Stober, was seriously injured and lost part of her right arm.

In March 1992 a large number of smuggled birds as well as two species of monkeys were confiscated on the Caribbean island of Grenada by government authorities. The Cincinnati Zoo sent Aviculture Area Supervisor, Dave Oehler, to help provide care for the animals. Oehler later arranged shipment for many of the animals to the Zoo and other facilities in the U.S.A.

Shoebill Stork. This large, rare African stork gets its name from its unusual bill which it uses to capture large fish and other prey.

Gary Denzler and Harris hawk. Educational shows and demonstrations inform hundreds of thousands of people annually about wildlife and conservation.

Zoo Education Grows

The importance of education in zoos expanded as worldwide threats to wilderness and wildlife grew and the environmental movement developed. Education and its place in conservation has become a critical role for modern zoos. Through the 1980s the Cincinnati Zoo's Education Department developed in size and in scope, creating awareness, providing information, and encouraging involvement. A variety of school, pre-school, and scout programs emerged, integrated by themes of the diversity and interdependence of life. Annual school visitation reached 210,000 in 1989 with 42,000 children given tours or demonstrations by trained volunteers. In the Outreach program staff and volunteers have brought the Zoo to dozens of schools and other groups. In 1980 Frisch's Discovery Center began live animal demonstrations for thousands of summer visitors. Later the Frisch's Animal Recreation Center was constructed to provide additional educational presentations. Nocturnal Adventures programs have given special overnight activities to thousands of children. Since 1985 the Education Department has also managed the renovated Children's Zoo. The Zoo's Graphics Department overhauled much of the Zoo's interpretive signage and graphics during this period. The Zoo's noted photographer, Ron Austing, produced outstanding photographs for varied educational programs and publications. An internship program for students from colleges and universities was begun in the 1980s to provide training and experience in a wide array of zoo operations and activities.

At the Zoo Amphitheater, R.C. Cola's Wildlife Theater has featured educational shows, including Gary Denzler's "World of Birds," Cathryn Hilker's "Cats, Cats, Cats," and Cecil Jackson's animal show. Their shows and demonstrations have annually informed hundreds of thousands of people about wildlife and conservation. Cathryn Hilker established a special relationship with one of her animals, a remarkably gentle female cheetah called "Angel." Through Hilker's educational programs Angel became one of the most popular of the Zoo's animals.

The Zoo's Education Department was awarded five AAZPA awards for outstanding achievement. One award in 1982 was for the long-playing public T.V. series, "Zoo, Zoo, Zoo," and another was for "Future In the Wild," an innovative program with the World Wildlife Fund in 1984 in which eighteen zoos later participated.

During the 1980s Thane Maynard became the Zoo's principal television and radio spokesman, appearing on a variety of local, national, and international programs. His local public T.V. programs on WCET, "Zoo, Zoo, Zoo" and "ZooLab" have been especially popular, while his public radio program, "90 Second-Naturalist," produced through WNKU-FM, has been syndicated nationally. A devoted advocate of zoo conservation programs and concerns, Maynard has developed a number of conservation programs at the Zoo. He has also worked as a liaison with other organizations and groups. In 1991 Maynard was appointed Director of Conservation.

Through education zoos can provide the public with vital information and inspiration about conservation efforts and concerns worldwide. Although zoos are vitally involved in preserving endangered wildlife they can save only a small portion of the world's biodiversity. In order to advance conservation zoos must work with other organizations, institutions, and governmental agencies.

The Reptile House — America's oldest existing zoo building — and spring flowers. The Zoo's botanical collection harmoniously integrates architecture, public areas, and naturalistic exhibits. In April hundreds of thousands of spring bulbs create one of the nation's outstanding spring floral displays.

The Zoological Garden Becomes a Botanical Garden

Ever since the early efforts of Adolf Strauch and Albert Erkenbrecher there has been an underlying theme of the Cincinnati Zoo as a botanical garden throughout its long history. In the 1970s and 1980s the Zoo's botanical collection steadily grew and lush plantings became a more visible and significant part of the Zoo. The informal landscape harmoniously blended a wide variety of plants with animal exhibits, architecture, and public areas, giving the Zoo a unique character and sense of place. Naturalistic landscapes simulated the habitats of a number of the Zoo's exhibits from the Chinese forests of the red pandas to the Alaskan coast of the Pacific walruses. Special theme gardens developed throughout the Zoo grounds, including the Butterfly Garden, Dinosaur Garden, Native Plant Garden, and Winter Garden.

Since 1980 trained volunteers have given tours to garden clubs and other groups while many plants have been labeled for visitors. In August 1985 the Cincinnati Zoo hosted the Midwestern regional meeting of the American Association of Botanical Gardens and Arboreta. By 1986 the Cincinnati Zoo had received four national landscaping and grounds maintenance awards as it became known for its outstanding gardens and landscape.

To reflect the natural interdependence of animals and plants and to highlight its botanical collection and displays the Zoo changed its official name from the Cincinnati Zoological Garden to the Cincinnati Zoo and Botanical Garden on April 12, 1987. The name change was a part of Maruska's vision of extending the Zoo's collections and exhibits to the full range of the world's life forms. The change also echoed the Zoo's origins and the long-ago recommendations of Adolph Strauch in 1873 that the Cincinnati Zoological Garden be established as both a garden and as a zoo. The change to Zoo and Botanical Garden was not just in name only. The botanical collection rivals the animal collection in value and far exceeds it in number. By 1992 there were 3,000 plant species and cultivars, making the Zoo's combined animal and plant collections one of the largest living collections in the zoo world. The gardens and landscape are among the Midwest's best, while the spring floral displays are among the most outstanding in the nation. Extensive plant labeling now goes far beyond the Zoo's first tree labels that were set out in 1894. Other vital parts of the Botanical Garden functions are education, plant records, and research. In 1991 the Zoo hosted North American zoo horticulturists at the annual conference of the Association of Zoological Horticulture.

Zoo Conservation Research

The Zoo's research program began in 1981 with funds from the Everett W. Townsley Wildlife Research Fund, created by former Board President Carson Whiting and his wife Kay. Dr. Betsy Dresser, a reproductive physiologist, was appointed Director of Research. The research program started as a joint endeavor among the Zoo, the University of Cincinnati College of Medicine, and Kings Island Wild Animal Habitat. It was initially known as the Cincinnati Wildlife Research Federation and later renamed the Cincinnati Zoo Center for Reproduction of Endangered Wildlife or "CREW."

Surrogate mother eland and rare baby bongo. Through embryo transfer twin bongo calves were born one week apart at the Cincinnati Zoo: one to a surrogate bongo mother and one to a surrogate eland mother.

WORLD FIRSTS

1983: Birth of an eland antelope through nonsurgical embryo transfer, the first exotic animal produced through this procedure.

1984: Eland born following transfer of a frozen-thawed embryo, the first exotic animal produced from a frozen embryo.

1984: Rare bongo antelope born to surrogate eland mother, the first nonsurgical interspecies transfer.

1988: Birth of an embryo transfer eland calf from a split embryo or demi-embryo.

1988: Several endangered species of *Trillium* wildflowers reproduced through tissue culture.

1989: Endangered Indian desert cat born to a domestic cat surrogate, not only the world's first cat born from interspecies embryo transfer, but the first exotic cat born from *in vitro* fertilization.

CREW seeks to propagate and preserve the genetic diversity of wild species of animals and plants by focusing on reproduction research. CREW rose to prominence with its innovative approach to the use of biotechnology and for the resulting births of a variety of species. It has been perhaps best known for its embryo transfer work. One of the primary goals has been to develop methods for using common species of animals as surrogate mothers for rare or endangered species. This goal was first realized in 1984 when a rare bongo antelope calf was born to a common eland antelope surrogate mother following a successful nonsurgical embryo transfer. This was the world's first embryo transfer between two closely related but different exotic species. It attracted worldwide attention and the Zoo received a Significant Achievement Award from the AAZPA.

One of the most fascinating aspects of CREW is its "Frozen Zoo and Garden." Also known as the Cincinnati Zoo Wildlife Germplasm Bank, it has emerged as a central feature of the CREW program. In a process called cryopreservation, embryos, eggs, and sperm from animals and pollen, seeds, and meristematic tissue from plants are maintained in tanks of liquid nitrogen at temperatures of -196°C. These frozen cells, which are in a state of suspended animation, can later be thawed and brought to life by CREW researchers.

In 1986 CREW added the Plant Conservation Division to its research program. A major focus has been cryopreserving hard-to-store plant species, many of which are endangered in the tropics. For this work researchers used seeds of cacao or chocolate to serve as a model. CREW has also applied innovative methods of plant propagation like tissue culture to rare plants such as the wildflower *Trillium*. To preserve the genetic material of native plants, CREW has also established a frozen seed bank for species endangered in Ohio.

During its first decade CREW has reached outward, educating others about its mission and integrating its research into the larger community of plant and animal conservation. At the Carl H. Lindner, Jr., Family Center for Reproduction of Endangered Wildlife facility, which opened in 1991, researchers share their work with both Zoo visitors and fellow scientists, while, beyond the Zoo, CREW International collaborates with other scientists to carry out conservation field projects throughout the world.

Dr. Betsy Dresser and the "Frozen Zoo and Garden." Dr. Dresser has energetically directed the Zoo's Research Department since 1981. The "Frozen Zoo and Garden" is a repository of frozen wildlife reproduction cells.

Test-tube plants are grown from tissue culture in a sterile medium. They are propagated for plant conservation as well as cryopreservation studies.

"Zoo Babies." Each June a special event, called "Zoo Babies," features the Zoo's current crop of baby animals. These rusty spotted cats are a highly endangered species and very rare in zoos. These kittens, born in 1986, were the first of this species born in North America.

"Zoo Babies" developed into an annual event in early summer, featuring the Zoo's current crop of baby animals. In 1987 the "Spring Floral Festival" began, highlighting the Zoo and Botanical Garden's outstanding spring floral displays.

In the summer of 1989 a "Month In Africa" was the first of a series of special events themed around a geographical region and focused on the wildlife of these areas. In following years these events have featured Asia, Latin America, and North America. They have included cultural and ethnographic activities, such as music, dance, handicrafts, and village marketplaces.

Sixteen years after the last Zoo Summer Opera season in 1971, music returned to the Zoo in 1987. The long-time Playland amusement rides, located behind the Nocturnal House, were removed and replaced with the Coors Peacock Pavilion. Here a summer season of "Jazzoo" began with popular music concerts that over the years featured nationally known performers, including Ray Charles, Tony Bennett, and Johnny Cash. This music facility at the Zoo recalls the old Summer Opera and the even earlier bandstands of long ago where German bands once played.

Zoo Marketing and Events

In order to keep up with the fast-paced fads and trends of popular culture, Marketing Director Glenn Ekey orchestrated a multifaceted marketing program that boosted Zoo attendance and revenues with a flurry of publicity, television and radio coverage, special events, and advertising. In 1988 Ekey left the Zoo to become Executive Director of the Zoological Society of the Roger Williams Zoo in Providence, Rhode Island. He was replaced by Shirley Bonekemper in 1989.

Throughout the 1980s Special Events Manager Donna M. Oehler, daughter of Director Ed Maruska, built up a series of special events, extending the Zoo's busy season throughout much of the year. She was appointed Director of Events and Promotions in 1990. The "Festival of Lights" grew to become a large-scale Christmas holiday event, attracting up to 160,000 people with its hundreds of thousands of sparkling lights and special seasonal attractions. Like the "Food Show" of years past, "Festival of Lights" has become an important community event.

"Festival of Lights." The "Festival of Lights" became a major Cincinnati winter holiday event in the 1980s with hundreds of thousands of sparkling lights and special seasonal attractions.

Volunteers have become increasingly important at the Zoo, serving in a variety of roles.

Zoo Support

Volunteers have become an increasingly important part of the Zoo's operations, functioning in a host of roles, from tour guiding to staffing the gift shop, the Children's Zoo, and special events. The Zoo has one of the largest groups of volunteers in the zoo world, numbering over 1,400 in 1992. Coming from all walks of life, these volunteers do multitudes of tasks that could never be accomplished otherwise, saving hundreds of thousands of dollars each year.

The Development Department, which began in 1977, expanded through the late 1980s and 1990s under the leadership of Nora Kelly and later James Thornton, allowing hundreds of supporters to aid the Zoo financially. Many donors continued to support their favorite animal's food bills through the ADOPT (Animals Depend On People Too) program. An annual series of gala fund-raising parties called "Zoofari" began in 1981, highlighted by actor Jimmy Stewart and his wife, Gloria. The following year's event featured Marlin Perkins who was the host of television's "Wild Kingdom" and who

was Director Ed Maruska's early mentor. Through the generous support of hundreds of volunteers, donors, and patrons these events have annually raised crucial funds for important Zoo projects. The Andrew Erkenbrecher Society honors the founder of the Zoo, and was organized in 1985 for major patrons of the Zoo. The Futures Society was also started in 1985 to allow individuals to support the Zoo's future through estate planning. In 1987 the Young Friends of the Zoo was established to involve young adults in a variety of Zoo activities.

Members of Cincinnati's business community, from international giants such as the Procter and Gamble Company to the smallest local enterprises, have been a crucial source of support to the Zoo through the Annual Fund, capital campaign, and in-kind donations. In 1990 the Zoo's largest capital campaign solicitation was completed, co-chaired by Paul W. Christensen, Jr., and Dwight H. Hibbard, reaching a goal of almost $15,000,000.

Red-eyed Frog. In recent years frog and salamander populations have drastically decreased throughout the world because of human activities. Because of their soft moist skin many amphibians are easily affected by environmental changes.

The Board of Trustees

The Board of Trustees has given the Zoo tremendous direction and assistance, donating thousands of hours of valuable time to support planning and development programs. Presidents William L. Blum, Sally E. Christensen (Mrs. Paul W., Jr.), Lela E. Steele (Mrs. John S.), James K. Lewis, Phillip M. Meyers, Jr., and Herbert Middendorf have provided vital leadership. Long time Treasurer Willis K. Waterfield has given countless hours of financial direction and assistance. After the passage of the Hamilton County tax levies, the Board was expanded by three trustees appointed by the Hamilton County Commissioners. Three members are named by the mayor of Cincinnati. There are now thirty trustees who serve rotating three-year terms. In addition, three Hamilton County Commissioners and three City of Cincinnati Park Board Commissioners serve as honorary trustees. Trustees serve on a variety of Board committees which work with a number of professionals and volunteers.

Former Board of Trustees President William L. Blum, Zoo Director Ed Maruska, and a young Bengal tiger.

Insect interaction. Young Zoo visitors meet a Hercules beetle held by Curator of Invertebrates Milan Busching.

Zoo Personnel

Under Sol Stephan in 1890 the Zoo employed fewer than ten full-time people. Today it is a sophisticated institution employing over one hundred and thirty full-time people and over one hundred seasonal employees in a number of departments. The Cincinnati Zoo's growth reflects the increasing complexity of modern zoos. According to Zoo Director Ed Maruska, "In many ways, directing a zoo is like being the mayor of a small city. There are sewer systems to maintain, roadways to resurface, a school to manage, buildings to repair, and a unique population to accommodate."

Ed Maruska has been the driving force behind the Zoo's progress. He has instilled in the Zoo staff a work ethic of hard work, high expectations, ongoing progress, vigilant animal care, and a priority on aesthetics, cleanliness, and maintenance. During the 1980s a variety of the Zoo's departments, including education, research, marketing, special events, development, maintenance, and horticulture, as well as the animal department, grew in size and scope to fulfill the needs of a leading modern zoo. Maruska has given department heads and senior staff a great deal of independence, encouraging creativity and initiative. His common sense approach to management, intuitive wisdom, and decisive quick-to-act style have been crucial to the Cincinnati Zoo's success. In the late 1980s Maruska was awarded honorary doctor of science degrees by both Xavier University and the University of Cincinnati.

Attendance Reaches a Million

Through the 1980s the Cincinnati Zoo was considered one of the top ten tourist attractions in Ohio. Attendance at the Cincinnati Zoo was remarkable when compared with zoo attendance in other cities of comparable size. Attendance climbed from 969,000 in 1980 to reach 1,030,000 in 1984 after a month-long visit by a popular koala from the San Diego Zoo. Attendance peaked in 1988 at 1,403,220 because of the popular fall visit of the London Zoo's giant panda. A series of special events stretched the Zoo's busy season from late March to early January. Group sales brought in almost 100,000 visitors. Family memberships grew from 17,500 in 1980 to almost 42,000 in 1992, one of the largest in the country. Since it opened in 1875 more than 60 million people have visited the Cincinnati Zoo.

Cincinnati Zoo and Botanical Garden, 1993.

A Zoo with Character

Throughout the 1980s and the early 1990s the Cincinnati Zoo was a leader in the zoo world in a variety of areas including its exhibits, animal and plant collections as well as its education, research, marketing, and volunteer programs. This was accomplished with an operating budget of $10 million in 1990, which was relatively much smaller than the budgets of other outstanding large zoos.

The Cincinnati Zoo and Botanical Garden has created a distinctive charm in its blending of naturalistic exhibits, lush landscapes, and historic architecture. While many American zoos are looking more and more alike today, the Cincinnati Zoo, in its recent renovation, has developed a distinctive style, using in-house designers and local architects for the design of its exhibits, architecture, and landscape. Much of the construction and installation has been accomplished by the careful attention and detailing of Zoo personnel. Beyond its physical attractions, the Cincinnati Zoo has blended its underlying educational and scientific emphasis with the excitement of a variety of popular special events and educational activities to create a vibrant and appealing world-class zoo.

Komodo Dragon. Two Komodo monitor lizards, the largest lizards in the world, arrived in 1990 as a gift of the Indonesian government. When full grown, males may weigh up to 300 pounds.

A New Master Plan

In completing the 20th century renewal of the Cincinnati Zoo a new $15 million master plan was adopted in 1987, a collective effort by the Board, staff, and architects Glaser & Associates, Inc. In its comprehensive scope, the plan is reminiscent of the Zoo founders' far-sighted planning long ago. It will include the 1.7-acre "Jungle Trails" exhibit, featuring Asian and African primates in an outdoor simulated tropical landscape, scheduled to open in 1993. The Bird House, originally built as the Reptile House in 1937, will receive a large greenhouse aviary addition and modern new exhibits. The Aquarium, built in 1950, will be expanded with numerous new exhibits and a lush tropical river entrance display. Improvements in parking and visitor amenities will also be made.

The first project on the Master Plan to be completed was the Kahn's Star Bank Exhibit Building, displaying the Komodo dragon monitor lizards, the world's largest lizards. In 1990 two animals arrived as a gift from the Indonesian government to the United States. The exhibit consists of a dramatic indoor enclosure with artificial rockwork, planters, and murals, as well as a spacious outdoor summer display area.

The Botanical Center, designed by McCollow &Associates, opened in July 1990. It highlights the other side of the living world, the plant life that all animals ultimately depend upon. The Botanical Center features seasonal plant displays, bonsai, interpretive signage, information on educational programs, a volunteer interpretive station, and an adjacent Oriental Garden. The Center was a bequest of Miss Lena Suter, whose German-born father had sung with German choral groups at the Zoo in the early 1900s. In 1991 the Zoo's Amphitheater, originally built in 1950, was renovated to create a new and exciting backdrop for the many shows and demonstrations held there annually.

October 3, 1991, marked the formal dedication of the Carl H. Lindner, Jr., Family Center for Reproduction of Endangered Wildlife. The $3.5 million state-of-the-art building has enabled CREW to greatly expand its research work in size and scale.

The CREW Center has been compared to the Ark of long ago, a place dedicated to saving animals and plants threatened with extinction. The building has holding space for animals ranging in size from mice to small antelope, in addition to an animal medical suite, a greenhouse and tissue culture laboratory, and a cryopreservation lab, the "Frozen Zoo and Garden," which stores the reproduction cells of endangered species. The facility, designed by Glaser Associates, is unique in the world, not just for the research carried on within its walls, but for its dual role as an education center. Its glass-walled laboratories allow touring visitors to get a behind-the-scenes look at CREW's work, while a permanent public exhibit uses a variety of interactive teaching tools to describe CREW's role within the larger world of animal and plant conservation.

The Carl H. Lindner, Jr., Family Center for Reproduction of Endangered Wildlife, dedicated in 1991, uses the latest technology to preserve endangered species of plants and animals.

Today the world's natural areas and its plants and animals are rapidly dwindling through human development. Wildlife is suffering tragic losses in population, genetic diversity, and species extinction. In the next century many wild animal and plant species will be able to exist only through carefully planned human intervention and management. Zoos and other similar institutions will play an important role in preserving many species that cannot survive under less protected and less intensively managed situations. Working together in a worldwide network of zoos and other conservation organizations, the Cincinnati Zoo and Botanical Garden looks to the future, committed to the understanding and preservation of wildlife and the natural world.

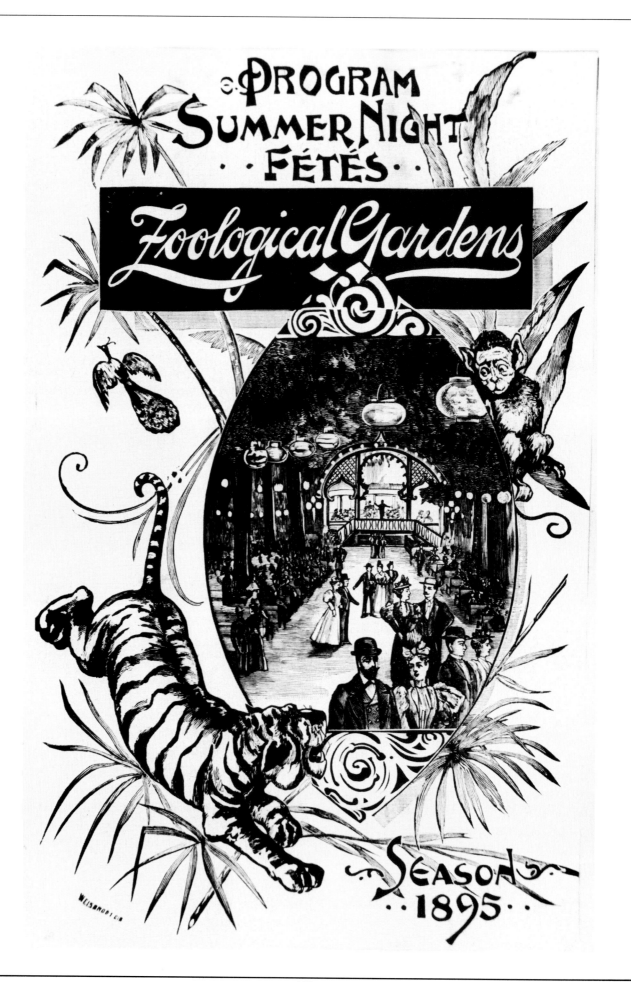

Program
Summer Night
Fêtes

Zoological Gardens

Season
1895

WEISBRODT CO

Chronology of the History of the Cincinnati Zoo
1873-1993

July 11, 1873	The Zoological Society of Cincinnati incorporated.
September 24, 1874	Sixty-seven acres of Blakely Woods leased as the site for the Cincinnati Zoo.
October 5, 1874	The Zoo's design by German landscape gardener/engineer, Theodor Findeisen, approved and work immediately begun.
March-April 1875	The Zoo's Agent, Armin Tenner, studied European zoos and hired the Scientific Superintendent of the Hamburg Zoological Garden, Dr. H. Dorner, as Superintendent of the Cincinnati Zoo.
May 1875	Construction began on the Monkey House (now the Reptile House), Carnivora House, Bird Aviaries, and Bear Pits.
September 18, 1875	The Cincinnati Zoo opened its doors to the public.
September 1876	The Restaurant or "Clubhouse" completed.
June 13, 1877	A large California sea lion exhibit with pool opened.
Spring-summer 1877	An Indian rhinoceros on loan exhibited at the Zoo.
1878	A California sea lion born, evidently the first sea lion to be conceived and born in captivity. Several more were born, but none lived for more than a few months. The first pair of giraffes acquired. "Daisy" and "Abe" were among the Zoo's most popular animals for many years.
1880	A trumpeter swan hatched, apparently the first Zoo hatching of this species. Four passenger pigeons were also hatched.
July 20, 1882	An American bison born, apparently one of the first born in captivity.
April 22, 1883	A young male Nile hippopotamus purchased. "Caliph" was later sold to New York's Central Park Zoo.
1884	A whooping crane exhibited.
1886	Sol A. Stephan appointed as Superintendent. He was the sixth Superintendent in twelve years. Stephan directed the Zoo's operations until 1937 (51 years).

1886	The Zoo sold 21 acres to a housing development syndicate to pay debts. A large new flight cage for birds of prey as well as other exhibits for buffalo, wolf, and prairie dog were built.
July 1, 1888	"Mr. and Mrs. Rooney," apparently the only chimpanzees in the U.S.A., acquired by the Zoo.
1889	The Zoo and surrounding area annexed by the city of Cincinnati.
October 20, 1889	The first giraffe born in the Western Hemisphere born at the Zoo. It died five days later.
December 15, 1889	Two polar bears born but died shortly after birth.
1896	The Cincinnati public schools began sending school children to the Zoo twice each year.
Jan. 22, 1898	The Zoological Society went into receivership because of indebtedness and the effects of a depression.
1899	The Cincinnati Zoological Company organized to operate the Zoo on a nonprofit basis.
November 1901	The Cincinnati Traction Company bought controlling stock in the Zoo, operating it on a nonprofit basis.
1902	"Zee-koe," a baby male hippopotamus purchased from the Hagenbeck firm. He died in 1923 and is mounted at the Field Museum of Natural History in Chicago.
1903	The three-acre Buffalo Range built for the Zoo's large bison herd.
1905	The first Przewalski's horses to be exhibited in the United States, acquired by the Cincinnati Zoo from New York's Bronx Zoo.
November 1905- May 1906	Joe Stephan, the son of Superintendent Stephan, went to Hamburg, Germany with Lorenz Hagenbeck to learn about the Hagenbeck firm's operations. He visited European zoos with Hagenbeck and traveled to Arabia and Africa on a large camel shipping expedition for the Hagenbeck firm.
1906	The Elephant House, then called the Herbivora Building, opened. One of the largest zoo buildings in the world, listed on the National Register of Historic Places since 1975.
1910	The Zoo's Abyssinian ground hornbill, "Jack," died. He was almost 40 years old.
October 17, 1912	Cincinnati's oldest surviving building, the Kemper Log House, dedicated at the Zoo as a historical exhibit. Originally constructed in 1804, it was brought to the Zoo in April 1912. It remained at the Zoo until 1981.
September 1, 1914	"Martha," the world's last surviving passenger pigeon, died at 1:00 p.m. at the Zoo.
May 1, 1917	Mrs. Anna Sinton Taft and Mrs. Mary M. Emery purchased the Zoo for $250,000. The Cincinnati Zoological Park Association was organized as a nonprofit corporation. Charles Phelps Taft, Mrs. Taft's husband, became the Board President.
February 21, 1918	The world's last surviving Carolina parakeet, "Incas," died at the Zoo.

June 20, 1920	The Cincinnati Summer Opera, better known as the Zoo Opera, started at the Zoo.
1923	The Zoo acquired an American alligator which had been raised from a hatchling by a Cincinnati family. Almost seventy years later, "Tojo" was recognized as the oldest alligator in captivity.
April 9, 1923	The Zoo purchased a female Indian rhino from the Hagenbeck firm for $10,000.
September 18, 1925	The Zoo celebrated its 50th birthday.
1930	Monkey Island built next to the Monkey House (now the Reptile House).
June 11, 1931	The Zoo's first gorilla, "Susie," arrived at the Zoo. She arrived in the United States in 1929 on the Graf Zeppelin.
September 19, 1931	"Gimpy," a baby "pygmy" African forest elephant, given to the Zoo by Judge Alfred K. Nippert. After twenty years Gimpy still weighed only 2,500 lbs. (compared with a normal 7,000-9,000-lb. adult female).
March 11, 1932	The new Zoological Society of Cincinnati incorporated.
June 3, 1933	The newly organized Zoological Society of Cincinnati began the management and operation of the Zoo.
November 3, 1932	The Zoo formally transferred to the City of Cincinnati after being purchased for $325,000.
November 26, 1932	Contract signed between the Zoological Society and the City's Board of Park Commissioners to operate the Zoo.
January 1, 1933	Newly organized Zoological Society of Cincinnati began the management and operation of the Zoo.
May 26, 1934	Barless lion and tiger grottos, designed by the Hagenbeck firm of Hamburg, Germany, opened at a cost of $2,500. It was the first of several Depression-era exhibits built through federal and private funding.
1935	John F. ("Jack") Heusser became Director.
July 9, 1935	The African Veldt exhibit opened after a dedication ceremony the previous year. Designed by the Hagenbeck firm, it was a naturalistic display of zebras, antelopes, and birds.
May 2, 1937	The Reptile House opened at a cost of $135,000. In 1951 it was converted into the Bird House.
May 9, 1937	The barless bear exhibits, designed by the Hagenbeck firm, opened at a cost of $104,000.
1937-1938	The old Clubhouse restaurant, built in 1876, razed in April 1937 and the Children's Zoo built on the site. A new Moderne or Art Moderne-style restaurant opened August 28, 1938. It is the Zoo's restaurant of today.
September 18, 1937	Sol A. Stephan retired at the age of 88 after directing Zoo operations for 51 years.
1942	The hoofed animal exhibit near the Vine Street pedestrian entrance opened after extensive renovation. It was called the "Deer Line" for many years. Edward ("Eddie") Coyne, an outstanding long time keeper and elephant trainer, died at the age of 75 after 65 years of employment.

October 29, 1947	"Susie," the Zoo's popular gorilla, died at the age of 22. She was then the oldest gorilla in captivity.
October 28, 1949	Sol A. Stephan died at the age of 100. He worked at the Zoo for 62 years and directed the Zoo for 51 years.
May 3, 1950	The original Carnivora House, built in 1875, demolished.
May 25, 1950	The Fleischmann Memorial Aquarium opened.
August 1950	A week-long Diamond Jubilee celebrated the 75th anniversary of the Zoo.
1951	The Ape House and the attached Amphitheater completed (June 9). The Monkey House, built in 1875, converted to the present Reptile House (completed June 14). The Reptile House, built in 1937, converted to the Bird House (completed June 15).
1952	"King Tut," a three-year-old, thirty-pound gorilla, arrived at the Zoo.
June 27, 1952	The new Carnivora Building opened at a cost of $250,000.
June 24, 1953	The Bird Aviaries, built in 1875, converted into monkey exhibits.
August 3, 1953	The Administration Building dedicated in memory of Fred Pagels, a German-born moving company owner.
1957	Dr. Albert Schweitzer donated a three-year-old lowland gorilla named "Penelope" to the children of Cincinnati. She was later given to the Zoo.
September 1, 1961	John F. ("Jack") Heusser retired as Director after 23 years. William Hoff became the new Director.
May 1962	The Walk-Through Flight Cage opened at a cost of $40,000.
June 1962	Ibex Island (originally Baboon Island) completed near the Ape House at a cost of $77,000.
August 1962	Monkey Island and the Vine Street pedestrian entrance renovated.
1963	The first caracal birth in the western hemisphere occurred at the Zoo.
1964	The Ape House nursery and the Nocturnal House opened; the Children's Zoo renovated.
February 29-March 4, 1964	The Zoo hosted the mid-winter meeting of the American Association of Zoological Parks and Aquariums.
March 22, 1964	The first crowned guenon monkey birth in captivity took place at the Zoo.
September 30, 1964	The third black rhino born at the Zoo.
1965	The Whiting Grove picnic area completed.
November 22, 1967	Director William Hoff resigned to become the Director of the St. Louis Zoo.

1968	The Goetz Animal Health Center constructed.
May 23, 1968	Edward J. Maruska appointed as Zoo Director.
March 1969	The penguin exhibit built in the Bird House.
June 8, 1969	The first sand cat birth in captivity occurred at the Zoo.
Fall 1969	The *Helios Guardians* sculpture by Michael Bigger dedicated in memory of Michael Grzimek, conservationist son of Frankfurt Zoo Director, Dr. Bernhard Grzimek.
December 9, 1969	A Persian leopard cub born by Caesarean section.
January 23, 1970	"Sam" the first gorilla born at the Zoo, followed eight days later by a second gorilla, "Samantha."
1970	A master plan for the Zoo adopted.
June 24, 1970	The first yellow-headed vulture hatching in captivity occurred at the Zoo.
July 1970	The Eagle Flight Cage opened, designed by Carl A. Strauss and Associates.
July 24, 1971	The last performance of the Cincinnati Summer Opera at the Zoo after 51 years.
1972	The Pheasant Flight Cages built below the Elephant House, replacing the bird of prey cages, built in 1886.
1973	Saltwater exhibits completed as an addition to the Fleischmann Aquarium.
March 1974	The Zoo's Education Department created.
April 1974	The Gibbon Islands exhibit opened.
June 21, 1974	The first three white tigers born at the Zoo.
July 18, 1974	The first pampas cat birth in captivity occurred at the Zoo.
1975	The Elephant House, Reptile House, and last remaining building of the original Aviaries listed on the National Register of Historic Places.
May 23, 1975	The Big Cat Canyon exhibit opened with the three white tigers born in 1974.
September 18, 1975	The Cincinnati Zoo was 100 years old.
September 1975	The Cincinnati Public Schools began an accredited high school vocational program at the Zoo.
1977	One of the original Aviary buildings relocated and opened as the Passenger Pigeon Memorial building. The first captive breeding of royal Goliath beetles. (The Zoo received the American Association of Zoological Parks and Aquariums Bean award in 1978 for this achievement, the first of several insect-breeding awards).

1978	The first successful hatching of smooth-fronted caimans in captivity.
May 3, 1978	The outdoor gorilla exhibit opened.
Summer 1978	The Zoo's Wildlife Theater animal demonstrations began with the "Cats, Cats, Cats" program.
August 5, 1978	The World of Insects building or the "Insectarium" opened.
September 1978	Director Edward J. Maruska elected President of the AAZPA. The annual AAZPA Exhibit Award awarded for Insect World as the best display in North America. The Zoo received two AAZPA Education Awards, the first of several zoo education awards.
October 29, 1978	The Zoo received the first of several national landscaping awards.
Fall 1978	Outdoor cat exhibits completed at the Carnivora House or Lion House.
1979	The Zoo's gift shop, the "Zoo Shop," opened along with other visitor facilities at the new Entry. First Texas blind salamanders hatched in captivity (AAZPA Bean award in 1980).
1980	The Frisch's Discovery Center opened.
February 28, 1980	The first aardvark twin birth in captivity occurred.
April 1980	The Cincinnati Zoo hosted the Great Lakes Regional meeting of the AAZPA.
September 1980	The Zoo received the AAZPA Bean Award for breeding Texas blind salamanders.
1981	The Research Department created and the first successful artificial insemination of an exotic feline species (Persian leopard) accomplished.
1982	The Cincinnati Zoo became the third United States zoo to utilize cryogenics, the storing of embryos, eggs, and semen by freezing. The Elephant House opened after extensive renovation. The Zoo given the 100-acre Anna L. Mast Farm to develop as a satellite breeding farm.
June 14, 1983	The first nonsurgical embryo transfer of an exotic species resulted in the birth of an eland antelope, "E.T."
May 31, 1984	A rare bongo antelope calf born to a surrogate eland in the first inter-species embryo transfer of an exotic animal.
October 14, 1984	First frozen exotic animal embryo transfer. An eland antelope calf born following the embryo transfer of a frozen-thawed embryo.
1985	The Andrew Erkenbrecher Society and the Futures Society started.
May-June 1985	The Red Panda exhibit opened and a renovated Monkey Island opened.
June 1985	The new Joseph H. Spaulding Children's Zoo opened. The Carnivora House renovated and renamed the "Cat House."

1986	The first Barrow's goldeneye and the first crimson rosella hatched in captivity at the Cincinnati Zoo.
April 7, 1986	The first successful captive birth of rusty spotted cats in North America took place at the Zoo.
October 1986	The Zoo hosted the African Rhino Workshop.
1987	A new Master Plan approved.
February 27, 1987	The Cincinnati Zoo designated as a National Historic Landmark.
April 12, 1987	The Cincinnati Zoological Garden renamed the Cincinnati Zoo and Botanical Garden.
June 1987	Coors Peacock Pavilion opened on the former Playland amusement ride site. The Walrus exhibit opened. The Crane exhibit next to the Red Panda exhibit and the Marsh Bird exhibit at African Veldt opened.
1988	First brown-hooded kingfisher hatched in captivity, first white-breasted kingfisher hatched in western hemisphere. Several rare species of *Trillium* wildflowers first produced through tissue culture.
July 22, 1988	The first exotic animal born from a split embryo, an eland antelope calf.
September-October 1988	The London Zoo's giant panda, "Chia-Chia," displayed at the Cincinnati Zoo for six weeks.
October 1988	The Zoo hosted the 5th World Conference on Breeding Endangered Species in Captivity.
March 1, 1989	An Indian desert cat born to a domestic cat surrogate, the first cat born from inter-species embryo transfer and the first cat born from *in vitro* fertilization.
May 1989	The first banded linsang born in captivity.
July 1989	The hoofed animal exhibits, called the "Deer Line," renovated and renamed Wildlife Canyon.
July 1990	The Komodo dragon monitor lizard exhibit opened.
July 18, 1990	The Botanical Center and Oriental Garden opened.
October 3, 1991	The Carl H. Lindner, Jr., Family Center for Reproduction of Endangered Wildlife, known as "CREW," dedicated.

Sol Stephan *was a pioneer among American zoo directors. He directed the operations of the Cincinnati Zoo from 1886 to 1937, retiring at the age of eighty-eight. The Zoo grew through his knowledge, skills, and determination.*

Cincinnati Zoo
Directors
and Superintendents
1875-1993

Dr. H. Dorner   April 24, 1875- May 2, 1876
(Superintendent)

H. P. Ingalls   January 8, 1877- Nov. 1, 1877
(Superintendent)

Frank J. Thompson   1878-1885
(Superintendent)

Salvator ("Sol") A. Stephan   1886-1937
(Superintendent, later General Manager)

John Seubert   1934-1935
(Managing Director)

John F. ("Jack") Heusser   1935-1961
(Executive Director)

William Hoff   July 1, 1961-November 1967
(Executive Director)

Edward J. Maruska   May 23, 1968-present (1993)
(Executive Director)

In its early years the Zoo had four temporary or interim superintendents who served brief time periods: Curt Terne-three months in the fall of 1874, Armin Tenner-less than three weeks in 1876, John Kearny-six months in 1876, and William Bebb-1885. Since 1886 Sol Stephan, Jack Heusser, and Edward Maruska have served for a total of 101 years of the Zoo's 118 years of operation (as of 1993). This continuity of leadership has created remarkable institutional stability for the Cincinnati Zoo.

Charles Phelps Taft *was a newspaper publisher and half-brother of President William Howard Taft. He was President of the Cincinnati Zoo Board from 1916 to 1923, the second-longest-serving Board President. As a young man Taft was the first Recording Secretary of the original Zoo Board of Directors in 1874. His wife, Anna Sinton Taft, and Mary M. Emery purchased the Zoo in 1916. (Courtesy of The Taft Museum- detail of* Charles Phelps Taft *by Raimundo de Madrazo)*

James A. Reilly *feeding lion cubs at the old Carnivora House. An executive of the Queen City Coal Company, he was the Zoo Board President from 1932 to 1950, the longest-serving Board President.*

Presidents of the Board of Directors/ Trustees
1873 - 1993

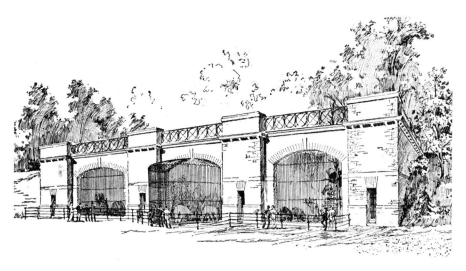

Bibliographical Notes

The archives of the Cincinnati Zoo and Botanical Garden have been the main resource for this history and include a variety of published and unpublished documents. Other major resources have been the archives of the Cincinnati Historical Society, the Public Library of Cincinnati and Hamilton County, and the Langsam Library of the University of Cincinnati. Additional information was gained from other institutions, personal interviews, correspondence, and other sources which are listed in the acknowledgements.

<u>Primary Sources</u>

Andress, Chas., comp. *The Barnum & Bailey Annual Route Book and Illustrated Tours.* Buffalo, N.Y.: Chas. Andress, 1906

Annual Report of the Business Manager of the Cincinnati Zoological Park. Cincinnati: 1920-1927.

Annual Report of the Zoological Society of Cincinnati. Cincinnati: 1874-1896,1934,1951-1991.

Cincinnati Zoological Company Board Reports. Cincinnati: 1905-1912.

Gordon, Clyde. "Happy Birthday Sol Stephan." *Parks and Recreation* (April 1947): 176-179.

M. Joblin & Co. *Cincinnati Past and Present.* Cincinnati: M. Joblin & Co., 1872

Leopold, Aldo. *A Sand County Almanac and Sketches Here and There.* New York: Oxford University Press, 1987.

Ratterman, H. A. *Cincinnati und Sein Deutschtum,* Cincinnati, 1901.

Shuvelt, R. *Supplement to the Scientific American,* vol. 82, no. 2116 (July 22, 1916).

Stephan, Sol. "The Passing of the Passenger Pigeon." *Game Stories,* Cincinnati, 1932.

Stephan, Sol G. "Sick Call." *Parks and Recreation* (December 1941): 157-162.

Tenner, Armin. *Cincinnati Sonst und Jetzt.* Cincinnati: Mecklenburg & Rosenthal, 1878.

"Your Cincinnati Zoo News," Cincinnati, 1952-1982.

Zipperlen, Adolph. "Geschichtlicher Ubriß der Entstehung und Entwickelung der Zoologischen Gärten." *Deutschen Literarischen Club von Cincinnati,* Cincinnati, 1880.

Zoo News, Cincinnati, 1983-1992.

Zoologische Garten, Der, vols. 15-43, Frankfurt am Main, Germany: 1874-1902.

Zoological Garden Pamphlets

"Album of the Zoological Garden of Cincinnati." Cincinnati: Krebs Lithography Company, circa 1885.

Guyer, Michael F. *How to Study the Animals at the Zoological Garden.* Cincinnati: University of Cincinnati, 1907.

"A Little Hand-Book of the Cincinnati Zoological Garden." Cincinnati: 1909.

Maruska, Edward J. "The Cincinnati Zoo Official Guide Book." Cincinnati: 1969.

McLean, Charles. "A Book About the Zoo." Cincinnati: 1893.

"The New Cincinnati Zoo." Cincinnati: 1942, revised 1958.

Stephan, S.A., ed., C.L. Williams, comp. "Studies in Zoology: The Cincinnati Zoological Garden." Cincinnati: 1900.

Stephan, Sol A. "Cincinnati Zoo Guide." Cincinnati: 1921.

Tenner, Armin. "The Zoo-Zoo." Cincinnati: 1876, 1877.

Workers of the Writers' Program of the Works Project Administration. "The Cincinnati Zoo." Cincinnati: The Zoological Society of Cincinnati, 1942.

"Zig-Zags at the Zoo: Unusual things you should know about the animals." Cincinnati: (1900-1915).

"Zoological Garden, Cincinnati, O." no publisher or date listed (probably 1878).

Newspapers:
The Cincinnati Commercial , 1873-1900
The Cincinnati Commercial Tribune
The Cincinnati Enquirer
The Cincinnati Post
The Cincinnati Times-Star
The Cleveland Plain Dealer
The Dayton Daily News
The Illustrated Buffalo Express (December 29, 1901)

Secondary Sources

Clubbe, John. *Cincinnati Observed: Architecture and History,* Columbus: Ohio State University Press, 1992.

Ehrlinger, David. "The Hagenbeck Legacy." *The International Zoo Yearbook,* London: 1990: 6-10.

Ehrlinger, David. "Considerations in Hagenbeck Design." *Annual Proceedings-Association of Zoological Parks and Aquariums,* 1990: 146-153.

Gale, Oliver M. "The Cincinnati Zoo - One Hundred Years of Trial and Triumph." *Cincinnati Historical Society Bulletin* vol. 32 (Winter 1974): 88-119.

Holliday, Joseph E. "Grand Opera Comes to the Zoo." *Cincinnati Historical Society Bulletin,* vol. 30, no. 1 (Spring 1972): 7-20.

Hutton, Mary Ellyn. "Cincinnati Opera: 1920-1990." *Opera Monthly,* (June 1990).

Meyn, Susan Labry, "Who's Who: The 1896 Sicangu Sioux Visit to the Cincinnati Zoological Gardens." *Museum Anthropology,* Vol. 16, No. 2 (June 1992): 21-26.

Spraul-Schmidt, Judith. "Other Beauties of Nature... Cincinnati and Its Zoological Garden, 1870-1900." Paper presented to the Cincinnati Historical Society, (October 8, 1980), (unpublished).

Spraul-Schmidt, Judith, "The Late Nineteenth Century City and Its Cultural Institutions: The Cincinnati Zoological Garden, 1873-1898." Masters thesis, University of Cincinnati, 1977.

For Additional Reading

Bridges, William. *A Gathering of Animals*. New York: Harper & Row, 1974.

Fisher, James. *Zoos of the World, The Story of Animals in Captivity*. Garden City, N.Y.: The Natural History Press, 1967.

Ford, Henry A. and Kate B. *History of Cincinnati, Ohio*. Los Angeles: Williams and Co., 1881.

Hagenbeck, Carl. *Beasts and Men*. London: Longmans, Green, and Co., 1909.

Hagenbeck, Lorenz. *Animals Are My Life*. London: The Bodley Head, 1956.

Hancocks, David. *Animals and Architecture*. New York: Praeger Publishers, 1971.

Horowitz, Helen Lefkowitz. "The National Zoological Park: 'City of Refuge' or Zoo?" *Records of the Columbia Historical Society*, edited by J. Kirkpatrick Flack. Washington D.C.: University Press of Virginia, 1989.

Klös, Heinz-Georg. *Zoological Gardens of Berlin*. H. Heenemann GmbH & Co, revised 1984.

Klös, Heinz-Georg and Ursula. *Der Berliner Zoo im Spiegel seiner Bauten 1841-1989*. Berlin: Zoologischer Garten Berlin, 1990.

Lincoln Park Zoological Society. "Celebrating 125 Years." *Zoo Review*. Chicago: Lincoln Park Zoological Society, Spring 1993.

Mergen, Alexa. *From Bison to Biopark, 100 Years of the National Zoo*. Washington, D.C.: Friends of the National Zoo, 1989.

Reichenbach, Herman. "Carl Hagenbeck's Tierpark and Modern Zoological Gardens." *Journal Society for the Bibliography of Natural History*. vol. 9, no. 4 (1980): 573-585.

Reichenbach, Herman. "A Tale of Two Zoos, The Hamburg Zoological Garden and Carl Hagenbeck's Tierpark." National Zoological Park Centennial Symposium, to be published.

Rosenthal, Mark A. "It Began With A Gift." "The Ark." vol. 4, no. 3, Chicago: Lincoln Park Zoological Garden, Chicago: 1976-77.

Stott, R. Jeffrey. "The American Idea of a Zoological Park: An Intellectual History." Ph. D. diss., University of California-Santa Barbara, 1981.

The Zoological Society of Philadelphia. *An Animal Garden In Fairmount Park*. Philadelphia: 1988.

Zuckerman, Solly, Baron. *Great Zoos of the World, Their Origins and Significance*. London: George Weidenfeld and Nicolson Ltd., 1980.

Photographic Credits

Index